Virginia H. McRae

The Phonogram

Vol. 3:3-4

Virginia H. McRae

The Phonogram
Vol. 3:3-4

ISBN/EAN: 9783741146152

Manufactured in Europe, USA, Canada, Australia, Japa

Cover: Foto ©Thomas Meinert / pixelio.de

Manufactured and distributed by brebook publishing software
(www.brebook.com)

Virginia H. McRae

The Phonogram

THE PHONOGRAM.

THE OFFICIAL ORGAN OF THE PHONOGRAPH COMPANIES OF THE UNITED STATES.

Entered at the New York Post-office as second-class matter.

VOL. 3.   MARCH AND APRIL, 1893.   NOS. 3-4.

TABLE OF CONTENTS.

NEW YORK PHONOGRAPH CO.,

257 FIFTH AVENUE, NEW YORK CITY.

SPECIAL NOTICE.

Phonographs and Graphophones for sale or on lease for business purposes, for home rent and for Exhibitions.

Automatic Nickel-in-the-Slot Phonographs for sale.

A large assortment of musical records of the finest quality constantly in stock.

Call and hear these instruments, or send for circulars and pamphlet.

THE COUNTING HOUSE
AND MERCHANT'S OFFICE.

A High-Class Illustrated Practical Journal of Commerce and the Arts, Devoted to Business Management and Methods, Shorthand and Typewriting.

Edited by A. ARTHUR READE.

Monthly, Price 15 Cents. . . . . . . Yearly, $1.22, Post free.

RAITHBY, LAWRENCE & CO., Ltd.,
London, 1 Imperial Buildings, Ludgate Circus, E. C., England.

Pope Leo XIII. and Monsignor Satolli. His Holiness Sends Greetings to American People through the Phonograph.

The Phonogram

The Official Organ of the Phonograph Companies of the U.S.

CANST THOU SEND LIGHTNINGS, THAT THEY MAY GO, AND SAY UNTO THEE HERE WE ARE?

The Phonograph Uniting the Nations.

As ages move on, the ties that bind the Eastern and Western hemispheres together are being continually strengthened and multiplied. Archæologists assert that the wildernesses of North and South America were first penetrated by hardy adventurers from Oriental climes, and that tribes from Northern Asia walked dry shod across the space separating that continent from North America, where now the arctic wind and wave sweep fiercely over the hidden crust that covers the globe.

Be that as it may, we know that many centuries before the Columbian discovery of America, Lieff Ericson, a daring Scandinavian, crossed the Atlantic, and swept with his eagle eye our whole Eastern seacoast.

After Columbus, came in quick succession bold captains with crews in search of treasure, and next, pilgrim bands seeking free shrines, and pioneers to plant new homes. Ere long, lines of vessels crossed the sea at measured intervals, till at last their white wings were found not sufficiently fleet to meet the growing demands of international intercourse, and Fulton set in motion an agent which now rules the world of commerce. Then came the electric pen which Morse used to conquer space, and finally our own Edison fills the measure of originality and inventive genius by finding a path for our voices across the trackless ocean.

Statesmen, diplomatists, financiers and the grand army of commerce use this mechanism to communicate with one another, but it is only within the past month that the Sovereign Pontiff, Pope Leo XIII., the ecclesiastical head of 195,000,000 of Christians, has transmitted a message through this medium.

We are informed that Mr. Stephen Moriarty, manager of the Edison-United Phonograph Co., which owns all the foreign patents to the phonograph, had a private audience with the Most Reverend Father, and delivered an address in Italian, congratulating him upon his Episcopal Jubilee. Mr. Moriarty entreated His Holiness to speak into the phonograph, and send a message of love and a blessing to the Catholics in America who would be present at the opening of the World's Fair in Chicago ; saying that this would be the first time in the history of the Church that the voice of the Sovereign Pontiff would be heard in America.

The Pope, bending over the phonograph

spoke into it; after which, turning to Mr. Moriarty, he said:

"I hand you this message. Guard it carefully, for it is the expression of my love for all the people of the United States."

The North American Phonograph Co., will exhibit this cylinder at the World's Fair.

The message to the people of the United States was couched in Latin, and by the Pope's special request will not be published before it has been reproduced in America. The message was then reproduced by the Pope's desire, and upon hearing it he said: "It is my voice—my very voice. This is indeed wonderful." His Holiness then explained to the Papal court that his voice would be heard long after his death.

Mr. Moriarty was also the bearer of two messages, one from the late Cardinal Manning and another from Cardinal Gibbons, of Baltimore; the latter asked the blessing of God upon the Pope. The Pope was greatly affected at hearing the voice of the dead Cardinal, brought, as it were, from the grave to his ears.

The Educational Phonograph at the World's Fair.

The Columbian Exposition affords the opportunity of seeing one great branch of human improvement fostered and stimulated by means of the Edison phonograph.

Mr. A. W. Clancy, the progressive and earnest chief of the educational department of the phonograph, will here present to the public examples of the benefits to be derived in employing this wonderful instrument.

Four sub-departments have been organized in this branch. The first embraces public school work, in which there are questions by the teachers in different studies, and responses on the part of the pupils recorded and reproduced, from various schools in the country, from the primary grades up to the high schools.

Second, there are declamations and recitations; also musical performances consisting of songs, quartettes and choruses.

Third, statements from prominent heads of institutions of learning, recorded on cylinders, referring to various methods of school work.

Fourth, a display of large numbers of cylinders upon which are recorded systems and exercises written in different languages—German, French, Latin, Spanish, Italian, etc. These show how the phonograph becomes an important factor in teaching correct pronunciation, not only instructing pupils in the grammar of their tongues, but repeating syllables and words indefinitely, until the ear of the pupil has become familiar with the sound.

Another interesting feature of the educational exposition is the collection of photographs upon the walls, where one may survey the faces and forms of those whose voices are heard in the recitations and musical performances.

The phonograph renders to youth of all ages valuable assistance, by frequent repetition of the vocabulary of their own or any foreign language. Mistakes of pronunciation are rectified by this means without fatigue on the part of the scholar or teacher.

That the phonograph facilitates the efforts of the educator in developing the youthful mind is now proven beyond cavil, but something more than a statement of this fact is necessary, in order to convey to the world at large a knowledge of the wide and important field of usefulness in which this instrument may be applied.

Paid His Backers Well.

The horse "Phonograph" came in first at the Elizabeth race track on April 13th, paying his backers five to one, and a handsome purse for his owner.

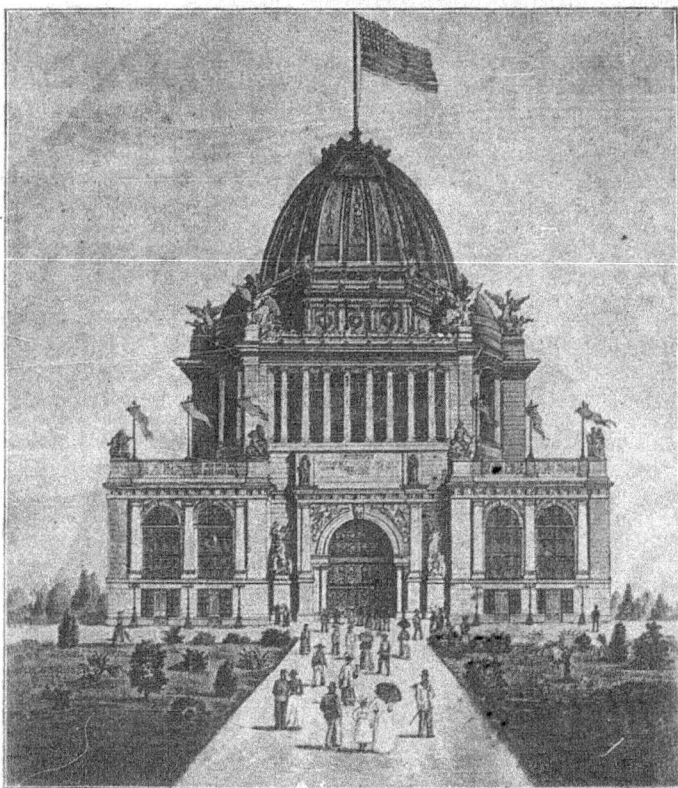

Administration Building.

The Columbian Era.

F. G. De Fontaine.

We are in the midst of an epoch that is all aflame with glory. While we may celebrate " the discovery of Columbus," that event sinks into insignificance when confronted by the grander achievements of human intellect that have followed. Our age is full of intellectual crystallization. Footsteps have grown into strides and strides into leaps and marches until we are tempted to pause and wonder whither they lead.

Watt gave us the steam engine; Stephenson, the locomotive; Fulton, the steamboat; Ericsson, the war ship with its revolving turrets; Franklin with his kite established the identity between lightning and electricity; Morse captured the vagrant element and put it in harness so that we may write and read thought as quickly as it can be flashed through space; Edison discovered that a thread of carbon produces the most effective electric light, and has so animated the dull iron and steel of machinery that it has become, in his phonograph, like a living voice giving back to us the records of a lifetime. Edison, Bell, Gray and other inventors have secured to the commercial world the blessings of the telephone. To Whitney's cotton gin we owe economy in the production of the staple that clothes the world. Woman bows to Elias Howe as the inventor of the sewing machine. The farmers of the great West remember Cyrus W. McCormick as the man whose genius enabled them to reap their vast wheat fields, while to William Thomas Morton Green, of Massachusetts, all the world owes tribute for his discovery of sulphuric ether as an anesthetic that has annulled pain in surgical operations and lifted the primeval curse of mankind.

These are but a few in the incidents of the progress of our age, but we shall appreciate them most when brought face to face with their grand results as they may be illustrated in the World's Fair at Chicago. We shall there be able to contrast the past with the present; the old with the new; the first rude steamboat with the floating palace of to-day; the locomotive that moved ten miles an hour with that which is now driven at ninety; the flintlock musket with its death-dealing successor that carries its own magazine; the slow going caravels of Columbus with the magnificent types of marine architecture, now moved by steam and fitted with all the appliances that modern knowledge can supply; in brief, we shall become acquainted with the human achievements in every department of thought and labor that have made this nineteenth century of ours stand apart from the others in its glory.

When the visitor reaches the Columbian Fair grounds at Chicago, one of the most attractive of its exhibits will be found in the Electricity Building. Here will be seen much of the work of that famous American whose monuments have already been erected, and, whom the Commissioner of Patents once described as "the young man who kept the path to the

Machinery Hall.

The Electrical Building—Front View.

Patent Office hot with his footsteps "—
Thomas A. Edison.

Among the special exhibits in this building, will be that of the North American Phonograph Co., embracing a space sixteen feet wide and ninety-four feet in length. The visitor will find it on the right hand side of the main stairway leading to the gallery. A screen made of turned and carved oak divides the space into several departments. One of these is for the conduct of the business of the company on the World's Fair Grounds. Another will be utilized for the exhibition of the domestic phonograph and to illustrate the social application of the instrument. In a third department will be exhibited the commercial phonograph with attendants present who will show how it saves time, that most autocratic of monarchs, and economizes labor in the offices of merchants, bankers and other business men. A fourth department will be devoted to the educational purposes of the phonograph, in which the method of teaching languages and elocution will be exemplified. There will also be a space enclosed by a glass structure in which will be placed a piano and certain special exhibits that will still further demonstrate the infinite uses to which this wonderful instrument may be applied.

These phonographs will be operated from electric light circuits and also from primary and secondary batteries. Possibly one may see there a machine for curing deafness. Wonders will not cease even on the spot. No machines are to be operated for revenue in the space alloted to the North American Co., but many coin-in-the-slot machines are likely to be scattered through the premises.

Among the attractions promised will be music, if not "from the spheres," at least from many of the great artists of the world, from famous orchestras and other organizations of whose performances in the flesh we only know by reading cold type. Here, we may close our eyes and imagine ourselves in the very atmosphere of genius. The voice of Mr. Edison will be heard as it "goes sounding down the corridors of time;" that of William Gladstone, will remind us of the "grand old man;" and there will be hundreds of others who are more or less known to fame at home and abroad, the echo of whose thoughts has been caught and imprisoned in this marvellous bit of mechanism whose heart of iron beats with almost human intelligence.

In the brief space which we can devote to the subject in this number of THE PHONOGRAM it is obviously impossible to enter largely into details. A volume would be needed to describe the astonishing effects that are contemplated, but it may be safely predicted that among all the exhibits in the World's Fair, none will be more calculated to stimulate the pride of the true American than these silent witnesses to the achievements of his countrymen—THOMAS A. EDISON.

Noble Edifices and Their Exhibits.

The Administration Building towers above all others comprehended in this scheme, as the Executive office overshadows all those sharing the duties and functions of government. A post-office is established within it for the convenience of employes of the Exposition, and a sub-station is located outside of the limits of the Fair grounds for the use of visitors.

This building is magnificently illuminated by electricity, and electric fountains toss their parti-colored spray to the air at the foot of the terrace on which it stands.

The liveliest interest is manifested in the Electrical Building, as it is the most wonderful. It covers five acres, is 690 by 325 feet in area, and cost $401,000. The nave extends the entire length of the building, 115 feet wide and 114 feet high; a series of galleries connected across the nave by two bridges, and reached from below by four grand staircases, form the second story. The exterior consists of a continuous line of Corinthian pilasters, which, including the base, rise to sixty

The Electrical Building—Side View.

Mines and Mining **Building.**

eight and one-half feet. A gigantic statue of Franklin is placed before the south entrance, and tablets containing names famous in electrical science are displayed upon the colonnade. The decorations composed of figures in relief illustrate the purpose of the exhibit.

The object to which the eye first turns on entering stands like the sun in the centre of a great system of surrounding lights, and like that luminary is so dazzling in its radiance as to cause all others to "pale their ineffectual fires."

Accurately described, it is a pavilion of glass. From the center of the roof shoots up a tall tower seventy-two feet in height; the whole a glittering edifice studded with incandescent lamps, which, with their vari-colored globes, throw into view, by kaleidoscopic changes, the hues of the rainbow. Surmounting this fairy-like structure, a powerful arc-light surrounded by prisms of cut glass to veil the intensity of its light, forms a crown of glory to the brilliant shaft and constitutes, as it were, a capstone to the glittering monument. It is impossible for words to convey an accurate idea of the splendor of this exhibit.

The illustration on the following page is taken from the *Electrical World*.

The American Institute of Electrical Engineers, at New York, secured through the co-operation of the authorities at the World's Fair two rooms adjoining the offices of the Electrical Building to be used as the headquarters of guests and foreign friends of the electrical profession, who desire to secure information or conduct correspondence while visiting the Columbian Exposition. The rooms are equipped with a long-distance telephone, and telegraph service and fire protection, and the authorities have promised to place one or more members of the Columbian guard at the headquarters. The American Institute of Electrical Engineers has placed in these rooms various objects of great scientific and historical interest; such as photographs, pictures, autographs, letters, rare electrical books, models, instruments, etc.

There are five buildings gathered in the group, of which Machinery Hall is the central and principal figure. Their united cost was $1,285,000, and they cover an area of seventeen acres.

Machinery Hall is 846 feet long and 482 wide; the annex 490 x 550, the power house 100 x 461, the pumping works 77 x 84, and the machine shop 146 x 250 feet. The main building is roofed by three arched trusses, presenting the appearance, in its interior, of three iron railroad train houses joined together, and having a height in the clear, at the highest point, of about two hundred feet. Around the four sides extends a gallery fifty feet wide ; down each of the long naves runs an elevated traveling crane, bearing platforms upon which visitors may sit and view the exhibit without effort. The fine coronas hanging from the trusses above emit streams of light. The central one, suspended directly over the clock tower that forms a striking point of interest in this display, consists of one hundred and two arc lights of two hundred candle-power. Each of the others contains seventy-six lights. The central corona is eighty-five feet in diameter, is star-shaped in form, and has seventeen points.

The design of this lighting system is due to Mr. Sargent, Mr. Pierce, and Mr. Luther Steiringer.

Among the numerous exhibits which appear in this hall, under Class H, its proper classification, will be found the famous Edison kinetograph.

The Hall of Mines and Mining is seven hundred feet long by three hundred in width. Its cost was $265,000, and it covers an area of five acres.

A portion of the exhibit in this building consists of marbles of various kinds and colors, which are incorporated in the building itself, as they serve as facings for the loggias on the first floor. Here may be seen ores of precious and baser metals, and their smelting and treatment will be illustrated by working models. The exhibit in this hall will be particularly complete in mineralogy and metallurgy. The most conspicuous is that made by Germany, in the center of the hall, composed of T and angle iron and an elaborate display of tubes and structural iron. The exhibit of terra cotta and stone for building material, as also coal, is very complete.

The United States Government Building, resembling the National Museum at Washington, has been erected for the exhibits of each of the departments of the Government, with a fine dome, three acres of area, and costing $400,000. Belonging to this exhibit is a battleship, moored in Lake Michigan, 348 feet long and 97 feet beam, which cost $100,000. It is classed as an annex to the Government building.

Half a million of dollars has been appropriated so far to invoke the aid of the muses in widening the scope of the Exposition.

The Music Hall and Choral Hall are devoted to musical purposes. All the bands, orchestras, choral societies, or in-

Government Building.

Electrical Tower in Electrical Building.

dividual musical celebrities in the world are invited to participate. Semi-weekly and semi-monthly choral concerts will be given. The Columbian Orchestra, which numbers one hundred and twenty members, will give daily concerts, and the permanent Columbian chorus, which is 2,500 strong, will fill in dates not otherwise engaged.

In the Woman's Building will be found, among other notable exhibits, the Crown laces lent by Queen Margherita of Italy. These will be guarded day and night, during the Exposition, by Italian sailors. No country has sent a finer collection of books than Italy, and this has been the result of the efforts of Mrs. Alice Howard Cady, an American journalist, who has long been a resident of Italy. She will appear as the representative of Italian literature in the World's Fair Congress.

A striking pavilion has been erected in the Woman's Building, draped with the flags of Spain and America, in which is displayed a magnificent folio of illuminated illustrations. It is entitled "Isabella and Columbus Immortal."

An enterprising young Armenian has been appointed by the Shah of Persia Imperial exhibitor for Persia at the World's Fair. Mr. Topakyan has had supervision of the erection of an ancient building which contains Persia's exhibits. Among the choice articles are an exquisite collection of palace and prayer rugs.

There is also an Indian settlement inhabited by Indians from Fort Rupert, Vancouver. It is comprised of four tribes of the Quachquhl nation. They will row one of their native canoes on the southern lagoon, and the women will manufacture baskets and trinkets during the holding of the Fair.

The admission tickets to the Chicago Exposition are printed on paper of heavy, durable quality, like bond paper in its composition. They are 2¼ x 4½ inches in size and are of four designs. Vignettes of Columbus, Washington, Lincoln, and an Indian in characteristic costume represent the four important periods of the history of America.

An arrangement for a corps of guides to do duty during the continuance of the Exposition is completed, and two hundred and fifty are appointed, twenty-five of whom are women. Their headquarters are at different points in the grounds, at which visitors can secure their services.

Ever Varying, Ever New.

Visitors at the World's Fair will have an opportunity of witnessing a novel spectacle in which the phonograph and the photograph play a dual part.

Before them will be displayed the faces and forms of a class of pupils in Chicago, taken by photograph, listening through the tubes of the phonograph to a recitation from a class in Milwaukee, a hundred miles distant.

This innovation on ancient school methods is wisely adopted. Any system that will induce precision and accuracy of enunciation will tend to prompt pupils to further efforts in memorizing their school tasks.

The general use of the phonograph as a reference for pupils is advantageous.

The American School Board Journal of Education, published at Milwaukee, in its March number gives the following facts in regard to the educational value of the phonograph. It says:

"Recent experiments have developed the fact that the phonograph has a definite educational value, and that at no distant time it will find its permanent place in the school-room. The many advantages which the phonograph combines are gradually attracting the attention of educators in all parts of the world.

One of the most significant facts is the use of the machine for educational exhibition purposes at the World's Fair.

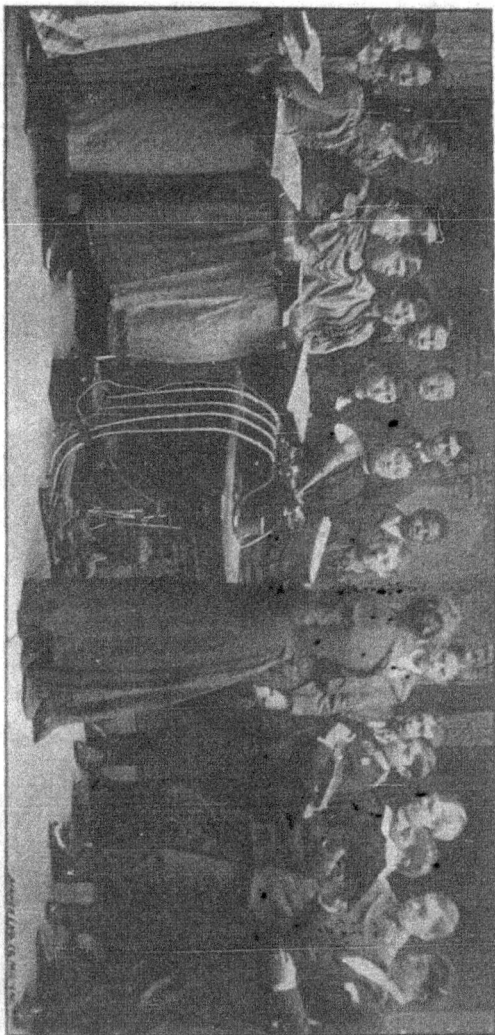

Group of Children Reciting to the Phonograph.

Steps have already been taken by boards of education to show to the visitor not only the results of the school-room as to writing, drawing, etc., but to present to the visitor class work and actual recitations as they are held in the school-room.

The uniqueness will at once become apparent when the visitor, after having examined specimens of penmanship, examples, in arithmetic, etc., finds himself confronted with a photograph showing the pupils, and a phonograph actually reproducing their voices in clear, distinct and natural tones.

In fact, the results of the school-room are brought to the visitor as closely and vividly as modern ingenuity is able to do this.

The phonograph not only produces every word that is spoken in the class room, but gives the voices in their individual naturalness and purity. Recent tests

made both at Milwaukee and Chicago have brought out some very interesting facts.

The children and teachers in one school are able to hear the class recitation of another school.

This record can be duplicated and reproduced on any phonograph. Thus the children of a Chicago class-room recently enjoyed the extreme novelty of listening to a class recitation of a Milwaukee school."

An illustration is given on the preceding page showing the taking of a record before a class of Milwaukee children under the direction of a teacher. A large receiving funnel or a number of receiving tubes is placed upon the machine and the sounds of the voices in the school room are transmitted upon wax cylinders. The

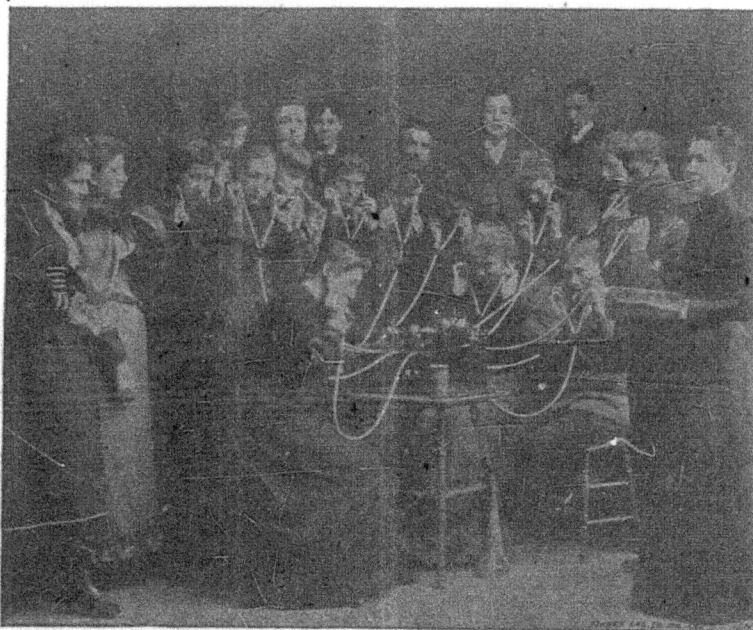

Listening to the Recitations of Scholars through the Phonograph.

are called "records" and show only slight indentations upon their surface.

They can be preserved for an indefinite time and used upon any phonograph.

The second illustration shows a class of Chicago children in the act of listening to the phonograph. They are delighted with what they hear in the school-room located a hundred miles away, and both surprised and pleased to learn that the Milwaukee children are as bright and well informed as they themselves.

The phonograph will be the means of securing an actual record of class-room work, from the songs of tender children in the kindergarten class to the declamations in the high school.

A Noted Record Maker, Dan Kelly, of Cincinnati, O.

We have obtained, in response to numerous calls from our readers, a very natural and characteristic portrait of Mr. Dan Kelly, of Cincinnati, who is so well known to all users of the phonograph through his "Pat Brady" series of Irish humorous records, and present it herewith, together with a short biographical notice of Mr. Kelly, which will be of interest to our readers.

Mr. Kelly was born in New York City January 22, 1842. His parents were both vocalists, from whom he inherited a peculiar and surprising vocal talent owing to its wonderful register, which, coupled with his mimicry, enables him to sing acceptably the heaviest bass or tenor vocal solos, negro plantation melodies, the Irish "As I's," "Come all Ye's," and "lamentations" in the true and peculiar style of each race.

His first appearance on the public stage was in Wyatt's Theatre, Hartford, Conn., in 1855, on which occasion he played the part of Paddy Miles in the Irish farce of "The Limerick Boy." Being then only thirteen years old, his impersonation of that character was doubly admired by press and public, from whom he received encomiums of praise. Preferring minstrelsy to the drama, he entered that line and remained several years singing with the best minstrel companies then in this country.

In 1871 he entered into partnership with the scenic artists Simmons & Morgan (the late Matt Morgan of artistic fame) to exhibit a panorama of Ireland, which was universally pronounced to be the best artistic production on that subject ever exhibited. The financial crash of 1873 came, the show business was generally paralyzed, and Mr. Kelly then withdrew from professional life, and afterwards returned to the boards in 1877, his last engagement being at the Buckingham Theatre, Louisville, Ky., in 1887.

At present Mr. Kelly spends his spare time in making records for The Ohio Phonograph Co., and writing songs, sketches and dramas for the profession. He commenced in the phonographic field about three years ago with Shakespearian recitations, and songs without accompaniment.

The idea occurred to him that an imitation of a scene in court which he witnessed when a boy, would be the thing for the phonograph. He immediately reproduced and recorded it on a cylinder, under the title of *"Pat Brady's plea in his own defense; a scene in the Police Court in Hartford, Conn., between Pat Brady, Mrs. Callahan and Judge Collier."* The record took well with the public, which encouraged Mr. Kelly to try other subjects; and he soon succeeded in placing before the patrons of the phonograph the celebrated "Pat Brady" series, which has been welcomed and enjoyed by the English speaking people of North America during the past three years.

Where is there a phonograph in the

United States or Canada without a Brady? The answer is, Nowhere! Wherever mankind appreciates the peculiar wit and humor of Irish character, that comical Irishman, Pat Brady, is always in demand, and it is not at all uncommon to see ladies and gentlemen standing in line before an automatic phonograph in many of our larger cities, awaiting their turn to hear him sing and talk. Mr. Kelly not only was the originator of these humorous phonographic records, but, notwithstanding his many imitators, stands to-day the acknowledged head of all humorous talkers for the phonograph. There are probably no records on sale that exceed these in demand.

Dan Kelly.

How Musical Records Are Made.

Entering the apartment represented in the following illustration, the eye beholds a scene so strange and unusual as to impress the beholder with the momentary delusion that he has penetrated into some chamber of necromancy belonging to mythical history.

Great demijohns, glass jars, storage and primary batteries, innumerable small-sized and curious looking boxes, embellished with tiny wheels, shafts, and governor balls, stand on all sides, while in the center of the room are placed two grand pianos, fronting which, at close range, pedestals or tripods are located, surmounted by huge funnels with open mouths ready to catch the sounds produced by the instruments. It will be seen the horns are manufactured with large apertures to receive sound, and taper off at the opposite end to a small tube, which has the effect of concentrating the vibrations and causing them to fall upon the cylinders with great force.

The interrogatory is often made to us, "What is a musical record." To which we reply, in technical language, it is the cylinder used upon the phonograph after it has received the almost impereptible undulations of the recording needle as it catches and transfers the sounds played from the instruments into t. The theory and operation of the phonograph are now well known to the public, but in order to define clearly the term "record," we will state that any cylinder upon which a succession of sounds has its intaglio representation is "record."

When a number of records are required of an especially popular composition, a dozen

the phonograph plays a concealed though important part. One of these is introduced in the picture in the shape of a phonographic doll—within whose tiny body a phonograph is concealed, by turning the crank of which the youthful image is made to repeat childish rhymes and nursery songs.

The making of musical records is an industry which has assumed enormous proportions, and special buildings have been set apart for this purpose. It is a

View of Room where Records are Taken. Edison Phonograph Works, Orange, N. J.

or more phonographs are ranged in a semi-circle around the piano and impressions are taken from the instrument through the funnels, a dozen at a time, and these are then duplicated by a secret process. The duplicates are as clear and excellent as the originals:

There are various mechanical wants contrived to amuse the public, in which

well-known fact that many excellent musicians have given up their normal profession to carry on this new art, as it is found to be more lucrative. Actors and actresses utilize their spare time in reciting and singing to the phonograph, and some very beautiful music is thus set before the public. This is a luxury to many who do not reside in the metropolis, where alone they would be enabled to listen to a Patti, a Paderewski, a Duse, or a Bernhardt.

The musical repertoire of the North American Phonograph Company is increased by this means, and the best talent is secured to furnish music for the people. Improvements are constantly being made

on board several crates of carrier pigeons consigned to the poultry show recently held in Madison Square Garden. Therefore many hearts had beaten quicker since the news came that several pigeons had appeared, two of which were captured in Connecticut and one in New

The Sinking Naronic.

to add to the clearness and volume of these records, and reports come in that they have attained a great degree of perfection.

The Phonograph at Sea.

In mid-winter, while tempests were raging over almost the entire world and the thermometer stood far below zero in many of the northern States, a stately vessel bearing a cargo of costly merchandise and precious lives, put out to sea from a European port, to traverse the icy and tempestuous main and reach a haven on the American coast.

Many of her kind had weathered the storm and arrived safely at last, though some met with irreparable losses en route, and valuable lives were swept from their decks and sacrificed to the fury of the waters. Holding these facts in view the friends of the fated steamer watched for her to appear, hoping against hope during the long period which elapsed since she became due. It was known that she had

York ; all being in an exhausted condition and eating and drinking ravenously, but although two of these birds had metal bands attached to their feet bearing the letter N inscribed on them, with the figures 7566 and 17601, it can only be surmised as yet that these came from the *Naronic.*

This steamer possessed one or more phonographs. What has become of these?

Fancy pictures the instrument thrown overboard as the vessel capsized, and sinking to the ocean's floor ; here, amid marine plants and shells, and surrounded by curious and wondering creatures of the piscatory tribe, its weird music reverberating through the aqueous element surrounding it, the electric sprite which dominates it impelling those notes to resound with unearthly melody, the magic mechanism discoursed to its audience.

" And strange unearthly creatures
  Make marvel of her hull,
  Where far below the gulfs of storm
  There is eternal lull."

However this be, we know that if several records of the condition of the disabled vessel had been made by some one on board capable of accomplishing this—before the danger became imminent, and these waxen cylinders had been placed in tin cases constructed so as to be corked like a bottle or jar, and sealed with rosin or any other preparation that would render them water-proof, these cases floating along in the path followed by nearly all the steamers crossing the Atlantic, would by this time have been discovered, and we should now be in possession of some meagre details of the terrible catastrophe ; or at any rate might gather from the records of those looking their doom in the face, facts going to suggest alterations in the equipment or arrangement of other transatlantic liners that would save them from similar casualty.

Expert Opinion.

Mr. E. V. Murphy, one of the official corps of the United States Senate, says that the phonograph will not only aid reporters to get out their work more cheaply, promptly and correctly in the first instance, but it will be comparatively light and easy to the labor of revision which is now so trying and difficult, and in an emergency will enable a single reporter to get out a much larger amount of matter.

Another Triumph for the Phonograph.

A correspondent writes : "The people have at last realized the advantages to be accrued from using the phonograph. In a few years no live business man will think of dictating correspondence to a stenographer. The phonograph will be loaded and ready for business while the stenographer is sharpening his pencil and getting his scratch book right side up."

The Phonograph's Strange Audience.

It's a Wise Man That Knows His Own Voice.

In a room in the Stock Exchange Building the other evening, were gathered a dozen gentlemen who were looking with interest at an object that stood in the middle of the group. It resembled somewhat a small horizontal engine. The spectators were guests who had been invited to an exhibition of Edison's perfected phonograph.

The electrical wizard's productions are all known in a general way, and the usual idea of the phonograph is that it can register human speech and reproduce it. Of the wonderful power and well-nigh limitless scope of this perfected instrument those present had not the faintest suspicion. They were, therefore, somewhat startled when the large reproducing funnel was placed before the phonograph and the cylinder was set in motion.

After numerous musical renditions of popular airs, Levy's favorite cornet solo, "Nearer, My God, to Thee," came forth in magnificent volume and execution It had been recorded by the North American Phonograph Company and sent from the laboratory at Orange, N. J. Then everybody was allowed to talk into the cylinder. It turned regularly, not saying a word, but faithfully recording every syllable uttered, with every tone and inflection. When all had delivered their little monologues, separate transmitters were given to each person present, and the reproduction of their words began.

All were acquainted with the different voices, and one of the gentlemen, far quicker than the rest to catch the different tones, told whose voice was being reproduced immediately upon each change. Half a dozen of the monologues had been repeated, when he exclaimed :

"There's an odd voice. Whose is it?"

A quiet laugh ran around the circle.

"I can't understand it," continued the gentleman, puzzled. "I know every one here, but I can't recognize this voice to save my life; I never heard it before."

"Are you sure?" they asked him.

"Positive; whose is it?"

"Your own," was the response.

And so it was. A curious thing about the human voice is the fact that when a man hears his own voice faithfully imitated he cannot recognize it.

Everything positively that relates to sound is under the control of the phonograph.

Is the Phonograph Difficult to Operate?

EMPHATICALLY NO. The little fellow who is listening to the phonograph through the ear-tubes, in the accompanying illustration, will be three years old in June. He is a great admirer of the machine, and can put on a cylinder, start the machine, adjust it, attach hearing tubes, and attend to all the details of reproducing musical and talking records, without any assistance or direction whatever. He has listened to many hundred different selections during the past year, and as he has "an ear for music," is familiar with all the popular pieces of the day, and can sing the airs and sometimes portions of the words of his favorite pieces, though his pronunciation of them is far from correct.

We have sometimes heard it said by parties contemplating the purchase or rental of a phonograph, "We would be delighted to have one at home for evening entertainment, but we fear we could never learn to operate it properly; it seems to be so complicated."

The experience of this little boy, and, no doubt, of many other children throughout the country, who are fortunate enough to live in a home where the phonograph is a member of the household (and the number is rapidly increasing), should be a sufficient answer to our inquiry. The little fellow's name is Philip Gilbert Andem, and he lives in Mount Auburn, Cincinnati, O.

Need of a Railway Annunciator.

A well-grounded complaint against railway guards in particular and metropolitan railway and horse-lines of cars in general is entered by the *Electrical Review* (March 18, 1893) in the matter of the absence of any means of furnishing passengers with a knowledge of their whereabouts as the train or car passes the stations on its route. The want of such an appliance has always been the fruitful cause of un-

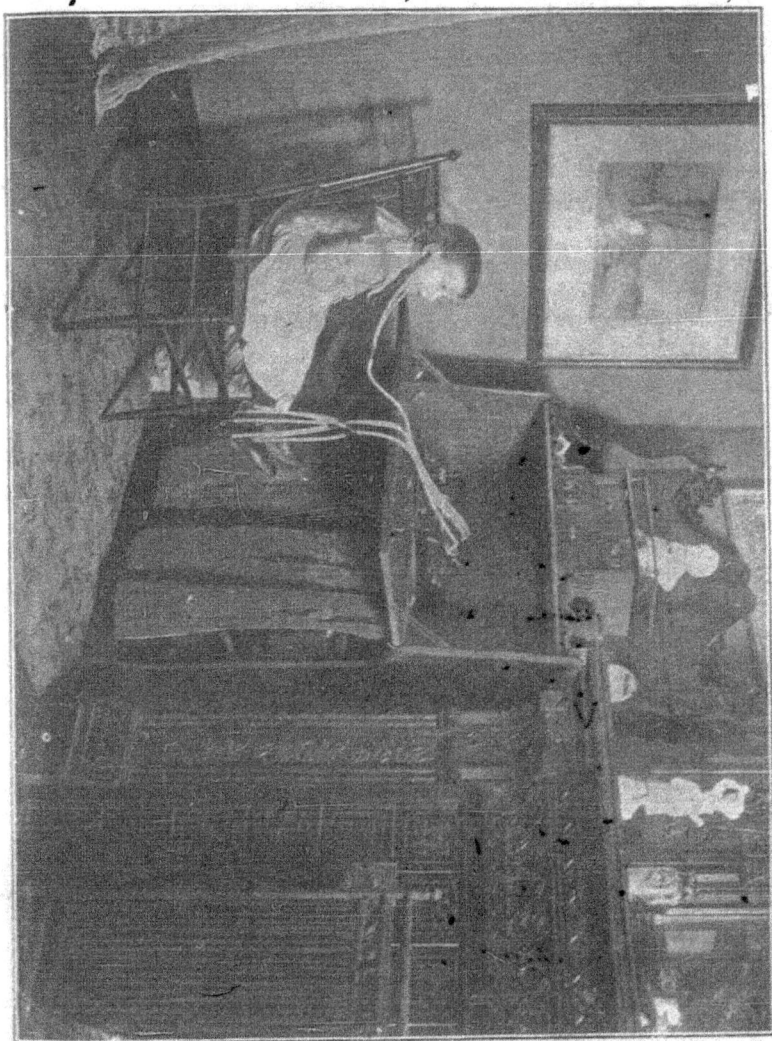

Master Philip Gilbert Anderson—A Young Expert on the Phonograph.

numbered misadventure, and of accidents resulting in financial losses, anxieties, sickness and fright. A remedy for such a state of things would be a boon to the human race and would be adopted instanter by every railway in the world.

The *Electrical Review* publishes on the same page with the above-mentioned article a notice of an invention which, cursorily examined, would seem to offer an appliance adequate to the desired end, but when analyzed is a sort of *lucus a non lucendo;* that is to say, it does not meet all the wants of the case.

In the Albany cars it may be easy to see a tablet with the name of a street printed on it, by reason of the fact that the cars are not always crowded and are probably not very long. But in New York the rule is the reverse in both instances; besides which, many passengers, who are aged, could not see any sign.

The proper method is to adopt a system of announcing the names, by means so entirely applicable to each passenger that its workings will never fail. What mechanism more capable of rendering this service than the Edison phonograph?

Testimonial From the Westinghouse Cable Company to the Phonograph.

The vice-president and general manager of this important and old-established house, Mr. Joseph W. Marsh, has addressed to Mr. Henry F. Gilg, manager of the Pittsburgh Typewriter Co., and agent for the North American Phonograph Company in that district, a communication on the subject of the phonograph which is couched in such well-chosen and commendatory terms, that we feel impelled to lay it before the public as an important witness in behalf of this instrument. He says:

PITTSBURGH, PA., March 13, 1893.
MR. HENRY F. GILG, Manager Pittsburgh Typewriter Co., City.

DEAR SIR:—Referring to your letter of March 13th, I take pleasure in saying that we have had two of your phonographs in use since last August, one in my office and the other in the stenographer's or transcriber's room.

When we first began the use of them, we had some annoying difficulties, due to our unfamiliarity with the machine, but by exercising a little patience, these difficulties gradually disappeared and for some months past I have had the greatest possible satisfaction with the use of the phonograph.

The phonograph saves a great deal of time for myself, as well as for the transcriber; in fact, without the use of the phonograph we should have to employ an additional stenographer.

While anyone who can operate a typewriter can readily learn to transcribe from the phonograph, my personal preference would be to employ a stenographer as transcriber, so that either method of dictation can be employed, according to circumstances.

I cheerfully recommend the phonograph as a valuable aid to all busy men.

Very truly yours,
J. W. MARSH, V. P. & G. M.

Cabinets Made for J. Pierpont Morgan.

The accompanying cuts represent new styles of cabinets designed for and adopted by Mr. J. Pierpont Morgan. They are models of artistic beauty and may, therefore, be introduced into the drawing-room if desired. Plate No. 1 shows the machine ready for use. The phonograph is so inserted as to be partly concealed, and the silver tubing is compactly arranged to afford facilities for eight or ten persons to listen at one time.

Plate No. 2 shows the cabinet closed.

Plate No. 3 is a cabinet designed to include musical records and contains ten drawers, each holding twelve records, which are classified.

All these cabinets can be furnished in

such woods as may be required by purchasers—ebony, mahogany, walnut or oak; and the models may vary in other details to suit the tastes of those who wish to acquire them.

With equal facility, but without pretension, and because its value has been so fully demonstrated as to silence questioning, the phonograph asserts its rights to a place in the counting-room or place of

Cabinet of J. Pierpont Morgan.—No. 1.

Change.

Nous avons changè tout cela, says one of Moliere's most famous characters ; airily upsetting with a few words a whole system in medicine.

business of literary, scientific and commercial circles.

True, it separates the typewriter and the dictator, but then the former really prefers a mechanical spokesman, and as for the latter, why his valuable services are much more profitable in other fields. The phonograph is usurping the position held for more than a past decade by the stenographer, but then these changes come in a sort of natural sequence whenever the demand for them is apparent, and the sale of typewriters will by no means be lessened, while the phonograph comes into its proper sphere. It is merely a case of the "survival of the fittest."

to them a knowledge of the great truths of Christianity.

The information reaches us through the columns of the *Methodist Recorder* and from the pen of Mr. J. F. Cowan, that the arduous labors of Mr. Klein, a missionary in Japan, should be relieved by the use of a phonograph. Mr. Cowan says:

Cabinet Closed.—No. 2.

The Phonograph in Missionary Work.

It is with pleasure that we learn of the important assistance rendered by the phonograph to the toiler in heathen lands who is trying to enlighten the benighted inhabitants of those far-off regions, by teaching them school-lore and imparting

Another thing comes to my mind just now. Intelligence from our missionaries in Nagoya, and a private communication which the writer received from Dr. Clark during his tour of missions in Japan, confirm the fact that Bro. Klein's health is in a very precarious state, and that he must have relief in some way from his arduous labors, or else he will break down entirely. Some time ago (and I hope Bro. Klein will pardon me for revealing the confidence) reading an article of mine in the *Morning Guide* upon my use of the phonograph in my editorial work as a labor-saving instrument, and later, after a conversation with Dr. Clark in reference to the same matter, Bro. Klein conceived the idea that the use of the phonograph in his school work and preaching and correspondence would be the blessed means of relieving what has proved a fearful strain, both upon his eyesight and his

in the shape of a competent assistant, or some such mechanical device as this, I fear it will be too late. If no one is willing to volunteer to go to Japan as a missionary, to relieve him of work and responsibility, why not use a phonograph as a missionary, to share his work and lengthen his usefulness to the church and the cause of Christ? Some Catholic friends recently did this for a priest in Santiego. Why should we not do as much for our laborers?

We trust these suggestions may find

Cabinet for Phonograph Records.—No. 3.

nerves, and wrote me some inquiries respecting prices and terms for the same.

Now I do not know that he will thank me for dragging his name into this matter and making this suggestion, but I feel like doing it upon my own responsibility. Why would it not be a happy and blessed thing for the Sunday-schools of our churches to make an offering of $150 by which to provide Bro. Klein with a phonograph, thus relieving the tension upon his nerves and his eyes, and, perhaps, prolong his life and services to the church for many years?

I drop this suggestion for what it is worth. If relief is not sent to him soon

favor with clergy and laity of this noble denomination and the sum necessary for acquiring the instrument be secured, for the purpose of presenting it to the weary missionary.

Improvements in **Phonograph** Records.

Every month brings with it a report from some quarter in which the phonograph has enacted a new role. The latest success achieved by it has been in the offices of the New York Phonograph Co., where the secretary, Mr. R. T.

Haines, has obtained a new class of musical records hitherto supposed to be beyond the reach of this instrument.

After various experiments, Mr. Haines has secured a new diaphragm that catches and repeats the upper notes of a "cantatrice" which have heretofore eluded the recording power. This gentleman, always on the qui-vive to widen the scope of his activities, surrounds himself with celebrities, musical, oratorical and scientific, who vie with each other in bringing out the latest properties of the phonograph. Among these are Mr. George B. Lull, formerly manager of the automatic department of the New York Phonograph Co., but who now has charge of the record department. Mr. Lull was for many years a professor of music at Poughkeepsie, N. Y., and he has through long experience and repeated trials come to understand how to accord to each singer and instrument their proper position in front of the horns. Their relative distance from the phonographs and from each other must be determined, and Mr. Lull's scientific knowledge of music and intuitive perception, render him specially fitted to this position. As a consequence the grating sounds that formerly issued from the wax cylinders, made by amateurs, are no longer observed, and the softest tones of the flute, the rich, deep vibrations of the bass viol, and the mellow, bell-like peal of wind instruments is conveyed to the ear of the listener, each distinct but none predominant. Truly art is a magic power.

The musical records that are now for sale by the New York company are far in advance of any previous ones, and we are not surprised that the sales resulting are equally large. The gifted artist, Miss Ella Thiebault, of Daly's troupe, sings to the phonograph many charming airs, although it was thought that the high and delicate notes of a woman's voice could not be distinctly recorded. The popular song, "Daddy Wouldn't Buy Me a Bow-Wow," which is interpreted with odd cries and ejaculations that are catching and effective by this favorite actress, has been in great demand.

Another beautiful composition of Reginald De Koven, "O Promise Me," as a cornet solo, was effective, played by members of Gilmore's band, as were also selections from the "Fencing Master" and the overture from the opera of "Semiramide."

Fact Stranger Than Fiction.

"If I could get five hundred men to agree to a like sacrifice I would give Edison one year of my life."

The speaker was an enthusiastic admirer of Edison's cleverest invention, the phonograph, and he was conversing to a group of interested spectators in the offices of the North American Phonograph Co. But he quickly added, "I should want to come back at the end of that time to see what he had done." It is indeed a wonderful little machine, that phonograph, faithfully reproducing words, sound, intonation of voice and all.

To the average mind this reproducing of sounds made weeks before is one of the strangest of the little machine's powers. But that this power should extend for years and centuries seems stranger still; yet it is a fact. The power to reproduce lasts as long as the cylinders are preserved. This has given rise to the clever idea which the manufacturers are putting into execution, namely; having noted singers and orators use the recorder and then duplicate the cylinders with the indentures to a thousand-fold. This is done easily and cheaply and the duplicates sold at a correspondingly low figure.

This idea, which has now culminated into a reality, gave rise to "phonograph parties" which have become a fad in the homes in the United States. A musicale at which the phonograph responds to the encores is not an uncommon event in society. In twenty years, the street fakir instead of carrying a bundle of papers containing chestnutty songs, will have strapped over his shoulder a basket full of phonograph cylinders bearing on their waxed surfaces the brightest gems of the operatic and concert stage.

Courting Phonographic Echoes.

Headquarters of the North American Phonograph Co., Edison Building, New York; Masonic Temple, Chicago.

The remarkable success of the phonograph brings the magician, Edison, again before the world, at this important epoch in the history of our country.

Edison Building, New York.

Some ten or more years ago, a group of visitors were listening to its musical reproductions in Mr. Edison's private office at his laboratory, in Orange, N. J. He dictated three hundred words to the wax cylinder, which was revolving at the rate of a hundred words a minute, while blue and purple flames were playing around the singing armatures. When the dictation was finished there was nothing visible to the naked eye to show that human words were engraved on the little roller. But the touch of a spring set the roller in motion, and this is what the active little machine reported :

"These lines are taken on the phonograph at the laboratory, Lewellyn Park, Orange. A number of gentlemen connected with the press came out to see the laboratory and the new machine. It is a great success, and it is the general opinion of all who have seen the machine this afternoon that the phonograph problem is solved."

It is ten years since that message was sent, and the history of the machine during that interval, as well as the magnificent exhibit now displayed at the Columbian Exposition, confirm the statement then reproduced from the waxen surface of the cylinder.

When this wonderful instrument was first

brought to the notice of mankind, it was treated as a curious, scientific toy, as the electric telegraph and the telephone had been before it. Nobody dreamed that the phonograph would ever possess a commercial value beyond that of a parlor rifle invention received from its inventor the thoughtful attention to which it was entitled. Turning it over with quizzical curiosity, he saw its slumbering forces, its hidden uses. A company was organized in England, advertisements of phono-

A Corner in Main Office of the North American Phonograph Co., New York.

or a bagatelle-board. The wizard of Menlo Park was too busy with other sorceries to give time to the development of the real resources of the phonograph, and he cast it aside as one of the little things with which he might while away a leisure hour. But the time came when the graphic wonders were cabled across to us, and Edison parted with the control of the foreign right, the American privilege being also absorbed by the North American Phonograph Co.

The handsome structure erected by the Edison General Electric Co., fronting

on Broad street and running through
to New street, New York, is the home of
finest electric plants for lighting ever
erected in this country. The offices of

Transcribing from Phonograph in Office of the North American Phonograph Co., New York.

this company. **The front of the** building
is of marble, terra cotta **and** brick, and in
the sub-basement is located **one of the**
the North American Phonograph Co.
are located **on the second floor of this**
building; they consist of the office.

for general business, the vice-president's private office, the treasurer's room, the parlor devoted to meetings of the Board of Directors, and an office set apart for the advertising department. The accompanying cuts give a view of a corner of the main office, where may be seen phonographs and typewriters in readiness for business purposes.

This office is an industrial hive in which a perpetual stream of visitors occupies the attention of the clerks.

The main office of the North American Phonograph Co., at Chicago, is in the fine structure known as Masonic Temple. The plate on page 382 shows the front view of this office, which is sixty feet in length by twenty in width, and is fitted up for the display of phonographs designed for commercial and social uses.

Other departments of the business are located elsewhere; the wareroom and shipping department on South Water street, the office and show room on State street, and the musical record department on Dickie

street. The phonograph is largely exploited in this part of the country. The educational department under Major Clancy, as we have stated, possesses great attraction for the public and also for the educational institutions of the country at large, and will play an important part at the World's Fair.

The officers of the North American Phonograph Co. are: Thomas A. Edison, president; A. O. Tate, vice-president;

Headquarters of the North American Phonograph Co., Masonic Temple, Chicago.

Thomas **R.** Lombard, general manager ; Cleveland **Walcott**, secretary ; Thomas Butler, treasurer, and **Scott** Tremaine, assistant treasurer.

ventor seem to have been unremittingly applied to the problem of how best to lighten the labors of toilers. To this end he studies the introaction of nature's

Thos. **A.** Edison, President **of the** North American Phonograph **Co.**

We presume among the millions of visitors to the Columbian Exposition there will scarce be one unacquainted with the name and fame of Thomas A. Edison.

The mental energies of the great in-

forces, making these his agents to cause movements in inert matter that accomplish what man alone has not the physical power to effect.

A man cannot speak so as to be heard at

f several hundred miles—nor a characters be transported f miles in a few minutes, ex- h the inventions of Mr. Edison.

therefore, the whole world owes a debt of gratitude.

The title of vice-president is frequently an empty honor, and the office it represents

A. O. Tate, Vice-President of the North American Phonograph Co.

s by the illuminating properties ty and indeed by all the various agency is made to enact, through gh comprehension and applica- s made of its energies. To him,

a sinecure; but in the case of Mr. Tate, who comes next to Mr. Edison in respon- sibility, it means that a trust has been be- stowed on a person known to possess those qualifications which guarantee efficiency and good judgment in the line of duties imposed upon him ; for Mr. Tate is a worker, both with hand and brain.

Mr. **Thomas R.** Lombard, the general manager of the North American Phonograph Co., holds an office whose sphere includes the business of this association both in New York and Chicago.

From the very foundation of the organization, his position has been a prominent and responsible one, and for this reason, as well as by reason of his talents, cultivation and mental superiority, he is particularly adapted to the post. It goes without saying that he brings to the duties of the office a vast experience in men and affairs.

Mr. Cleveland Walcott has been connected with the company since its organization, and his promotion to the office of secretary from a clerical position, is an

evidence of the appreciation of his excellent services by the company to whom he owes this well-deserved advancement.

The financial interests of the company are well managed by Mr. Thomas Butler, who is in charge of the department where fidelity and exactness are the qualifications most in demand. To secure the office of treasurer of an association of such import-

Front View of Office of the North American Phonograph Company, Chicago.

ance, one must merit the confidence thereby reposed.

He is ably assisted by Mr. Scott Tremaine, who was elected a director in the North American Phonograph Co. some two years ago, and was afterwards appointed auditor for the home office and the various sub-companies. During the present month the Board of Directors tendered to Mr. Tremaine the post of assistant treasurer, which he now holds.

Thomas R. Lombard, General Manager, North American Phonograph Co.

Musical Bulletins.

Weekly bulletins are issued by the North American Phonograph Co., at their building, No. 44 Broad street, New York, giving consecutive installments of new music recorded by their artists at the large building set apart for this purpose, 56 East Thirteenth street.

These comprise many beautiful and choice selections, of which the following are especially fine:

Clarionet solo, R. K. Franklin, soloist:

Selection from the Ballet of Mathias Sandorf.

"Old Folks at Home."

Vocal selections:

"Marguerite," Gounod, Ed Francis, tenor soloist.

Cleveland Walcott, Secretary, North American Phonograph Co.

"The Song that Touched My Heart," Ed Clarence, baritone soloist.

Points on the Automatic Reproducer.

We have received a great many queries about the "Automatic Reproducer," as it is called, and for the benefit of our readers we beg to set forth a few points in relation to the device.

It differs from the regular phonograph Speaker (or diaphragm) in the following:—

It has no recording stylus, and, owing

Thomas Butler, Treasurer, North American Phonograph Co.

Scott Tremaine, Assistant Treasurer, North American Phonograph Co.

to its form of construction, cannot be fitted with one.

The weight, which is much heavier and larger than that of a Speaker, is swung from the lower edge of the cup instead of from the upper, thus changing the fulcrum of the arm to which the sapphire reproducing ball is attached. Besides this change in its relative position the hinge at the point where the weight attaches to the cup is so arranged as to allow of a lateral or "wobbling" motion,

matic Reproducer obviates this little difficulty as it follows these irregularities without getting out of the track made by the recording stylus.

Our attention has been called to cases where this device failed to work automatically, and upon careful investigation of this *apparent* defect we find that it is almost always due to outside causes, such as dirt or gummed oil upon the sapphire arm and crosshead (the little brass disc which fastens to the diaphragm glass),

A Corner in Office of the North American Phonograph Company, Chicago.

the fulcrum sapphire arm having also considerable play from side to side. This loose-jointedness, as it might be called, allows the reproducer ball to drop into the groove made by the recorder without external aid and to remain there by its own pliability, even though there may be some irregularities in the record.

At times a great deal of trouble is experienced by the record of coin-slot machines getting out of adjustment, either through sudden changes of temperature or defective record-making. The Auto-

sometimes, also, its cause lies in the same trouble with the hinge of the weight. This gummy substance can be easily removed by using a small brush dipped in benzine, and good results can be obtained by the application of a very small amount of watch oil at these points, after thoroughly cleaning them as above. Care must be exercised, however, to avoid getting any of the oil upon the sapphire as it will cause dust to accumulate on the records and make the reproduction sound scratchy.

Some Facts Relating to the Early Development of the Phonograph.

BY O. K. DAVIS.

We print in this issue of THE PHONO-GRAM a group picture of seven men who rendered valuable services to Mr. Edison in the mechanical perfection of the phonograph. The photograph from which this picture was made was taken at the Edison laboratory in June, 1888. Mr. Edison is seated behind the table in the center. The men with him are Col. Geo. E. Gouraud, W. K. L. Dickson, A. Theo. E. Wangemann, Chas. Batchelder, Fred Ott, John F. Ott and C. H. Brown. Some of these had special duties to perform. Colonel Gouraud was acting as European agent, Dr. Wangemann was the musical expert, and had charge of the record department; W. K. L. Dickson, his artist, assisted by C. H. Brown, was a long and trusted lieutenant; Chas. Batchelder was the first manager of the factory where the perfected phonograph was made, and Fred Ott did a great deal of work in connection with the phonograph, his wonderful skill in the mechanical line making him one of Edison's favorites. They were associated with the wizard of electricity in his efforts to construct a machine which would reproduce the tones of the human voice exactly as they were uttered, with all niceties of articulation and inflection. At first they lacked something of the fervor which possessed the great inventor himself, but they had not been working with him very long before they all became imbued with the enthusiasm which inspired Edison, the zeal which nerves men for tremendous efforts, and enables them to sustain great and long continued strain. Edison himself seemed never to tire. His strength was derived from the peculiar inspiration which impels such men to conquer magnificent tasks. The infection of it so thoroughly possessed his

associates that often they worked for twenty-four and even fifty consecutive hours, and when at length they were overcome by fatigue which could no longer be fought off, they sometimes quietly sought nooks and corners of the laboratory and threw themselves down for the so greatly needed sleep.

It has been told of Edison that occasionally at such times he would leave the laboratory and hire a band to go back and play to his comrades until they were awakened. Sometimes, too, when his associates were so worn out that they felt they must go home for rest and sleep, Edison would lock the doors of the laboratory and tell them that they must stay until the work was completed.

It was while he was working in this fashion on the phonograph that a friend of Edison, who was visiting the great electrician at his laboratory, asked him what time it was. Edison replied that he did not know.

"Where's your watch?" asked his friend.

"Watch?" said Edison, "I never had any watch. I don't want to know how time goes."

Finally the phonograph was completed, imperfectly at first, but quickly improved. When it was finished and Edison had the machine which would reproduce the human voice, he wanted to try it by the voice of every human being he saw. One night when he went home he saw his baby, still a wee small chick, asleep in its crib, he caught up the child and hurried back to the laboratory with it bent on seeing how the phonograph would reproduce its cooing and its crying. But the baby had inherited too much of its father's good nature to assist at the experiment. It obstinately refused to cry until at last the inventor forgot his feeling for his child in his enthusiasm for his machine and began to pinch the baby. Mrs. Edison found him gleefully grinding out the baby's screams of pain and all unmindful of the baby and of the cause of its grief.

the great enthusiasm which dominated Thomas Alva Edison and which has resulted in the production of many mar-

W. K. L. Dickson. Chas. Batchelder. A. Theo. E. Wangemann. John F. Ott. C. A. Brown.
Fred Ott. T. A. Edison. Col. Geo. E. Gouraud.
Group of Night Workers, with Edison at the Phonograph.

The picture of this group of men is a memorable one. The men who compose it were the first to become inspired with

velous inventions which will go down to history as the wonders of the nineteenth century.

The Edison Phonograph in Canada.

Mr. A. Bryce, who has succeeded the Holland Brothers as agent for the Edison phonograph in Canada, writing from his section, says, in regard to the commercial machine : This hitherto neglected field of industry is now being pushed with vigor. The musical phonograph has for two years past attracted wide-spread attention and kept our entire force busy attending fairs, concerts, lectures, etc., where it was introduced as an especial feature. Recently, however, I have devoted my time to placing the commercial phonograph, and with great success.

I have just sold two commercial outfits to the general manager of the Grand Trunk Railway. There are twelve or fifteen firms who are waiting to hear the results of his experience with the instrument, before deciding to purchase. The assistant general manager, Mr. Percy, has already declared his intention of introducing it into all their principal offices, so pleased are they with results.

I must tell you of an interesting social organization that exists in Montreal, having for its object the acquisition and preservation of all literature and observances among the native population which tends to characterize the Frankish people. Its title is the "Folk Lore Society" and its mission is to take note of all customs, rites, etc., such as street cries and the like.

Many prominent citizens are at the head of this association, since it is not conducted merely as a source of amusement, but to aid in solving problems connected with biology and kindred sciences. I have recorded the street cries of every race and creed, which were given to me by this Society, and the cylinders containing them have been transmitted to Boston to be shown at the World's Fair in Chicago. I have also taken records of the principal speeches made at the celebrated McGill University of Canada, as also of the best songs of famous operatic artists who have appeared there.

The Missionary Society of the Wesleyan University are arranging to hold a meeting which will be addressed by missionaries from all parts of the world. I have been employed to take phonograph records of these speeches previous to their departure, and these farewell words will be despatched to all parts of Canada and reproduced from the phonograph by an agent, thus saving great labor, time and expense to the persons engaged in this noble work, who formerly were obliged personally to visit all the principal towns and cities in the Dominion.

Hungarian Telephonic News Service.

The Viennese correspondent of the *Standard* announces the appearance of a telephonic journal at Buda-Pesth. For the moderate sum of three francs (about seventy-five cents) per month, subscribers receive at their homes the latest political, local and commercial news, which are telephoned to them from the central office. This office (or bureau) conducts two services ; that of superintendence, which receives the telegraphic communications and classes them, and that of publication, where experienced operators transmit the bulk of the manuscripts that have been despatched to them from hour to hour Service begins at eight o'clock in the morning and continues till nine in the evening. This innovation will be greatly appreciated in the Hungarian capital.

THE PHONOGRAM adds this suggestion that in case of the absence of a subscriber, at the usual hour for dispatching the messages, all telephonic news could be recorded on phonographs conveniently placed to receive them in the homes of the patrons, and thus avoid much complication.

Shorthand Cripples Enemies to the Profession.

The following from the address of Dr. Karl Albrecht, before the International Shorthand Congress at Munich, is clipped from the *Phonographic World:*

"He who withholds unqualified persons from entering the stenographic field renders a greater service to our cause than courses. This kind of charlatanry will always result in delusions."

New Designs in Cabinets.

The cuts following represent new cabinets in which the phonograph may be inserted. They are a great improvement on those formerly manufactured. The

Phonograph Cabinet, No 1.

the teacher who mechanically turns out hundreds of shorthand cripples. Do not spread the idea that the acquirement of the art is a very easy thing. By so doing you are advocating an investment of time and money under false pretenses. You sin against the person as well as against the cause. Shorthand cripples are its most dangerous enemies, as they will naturally attribute their failure to 'insurmountable difficulties' of which they had not been aware. Such misrepresentations go hand in hand with so-called rapid

North American Phonograph Co. will make a large display of these cabinets in different woods at the Columbian Exposition.

The points of excellence are as follows : The body of the cabinet does not extend to the ground, but is mounted on carved legs and rises in an arch from one section to the other, thus preventing injury to that portion which formerly rested on the floor and was subject to being scraped by the feet of persons using it, or by the action of cleansing the floor.

The Phonogram Club.

This is a new and useful association founded by public-spirited citizens of Chicago, intended to promote a knowledge of the instrument from which it takes its name, to advance the interests of those persons who are members of the club and extend the use of the machine.

together persons who use the phonograph habitually, and by giving them such information concerning the purposes of the club and the work carried on as shall induce them to join.

The conditions of membership are that persons shall be practical operators of the phonograph, and exert their influence in securing additions of new members.

Phonograph Cabinet, No. 2.

This club was organized in February, 1893, and has had three regular monthly meetings and special meetings on every Friday evening since its inception.

It has now enrolled about forty members, and we are informed that many persons are seeking membership in its ranks.

A special function of this club is to aid in increasing the membership by bringing

In its social aspect the Phonogram Club is attractive, offering always entertainment of the most agreeable sort through its musical artists and imparting the latest information as to improved methods of operating and hints as to the care of the phonograph. The ladies are especially welcomed, and they make desirable members.

No plan could be better than that formed by this club to advance the interests of the instrument. Each member is an advertising agent who proclaims its merits, and often instructs in all matters essential to familiarity with it. The regular monthly meetings occur on the fourth Friday evening at eight o'clock, the session lasting from one to two hours. Weekly meetings are also held on Friday evening of each week, except on the evening designated for the monthly meeting. The officers consist of a president, vice-president, secretary, and treasurer. They hold office

An Admirable Statement of the Merits of the Phonograph.

Dr. J. F. Cowan, of Pittsburgh, Pa., whose labors in literary and professional fields are widely known and appreciated, expresses his views with regard to the phonograph very clearly in a letter to Mrs. Marietta Holley (Josiah Allen's wife), the popular authoress, of Adams, Jefferson County, N. Y., and we think his reasoning and statistics as to its qualities speak so highly in its favor that we give it in full.

A Natural Tie.

from the date of the election until January 1st of the year following.

THE PHONOGRAM has been declared their official organ, and is a welcome accession.

THE PHONOGRAM suggests that similar organizations be formed in other cities for the benefit of this art, just as the many stenographic associations have conduced greatly to the knowledge and introduction of shorthand. In this way they add to the strength of the association and exercise a powerful influence, and control matters affecting their special interests.

United by Common Interests.

The pretty engraving here shown is emblematic of the relations existing between the typewriter and the phonograph, which in the nature of things must remain indissoluble.

This letter was recently published in *The Financier*, the reliable and excellent journal devoted to all large interests from a financial standpoint, at No. 5 Broadway, N. Y. :

PITTSBURGH, PA., March 15, 1893.

MRS. MARIETTA HOLLEY,
Adams, Jefferson Co., N. Y.

DEAR MADAM :—Your favor of the 8th at hand and contents noted. First let me thank you for your kindness in answering the questions propounded to you. I have no doubt you are troubled with a great many solicitations, and it is exceedingly gracious in you to give attention to the matter.

In reference to the phonograph, allow me to enclose to you a printed slip, published some four or five months ago, setting forth my own methods of work and experience with the phonograph as a help in literary labor. In addition to what is therein stated, I am pleased to say that after a year's experience with the phonograph I have nothing to retract from my first statement, but rather I would add that it continues to prove the most welcome, time-saving, labor-saving and money-saving assistant I have ever employed in my work. I am still using two phonographs; one in my office in the city of Pittsburgh, and the other in my home in Beaver Falls, Pa., where I do most of my dictating, while the transcribing is done from the other instrument in the office. I do fifty per cent more work than I did when dictating to a stenographer. And whereas, a good stenographer cost me from $50.00 per month upwards, the services of a good typewriter, who needs no further technical knowledge to be able to transcribe from the phonograph than can be acquired in an hour's use of it, can be had from $20.00 to $30.00. The difference thus saved would soon pay for the instrument.

In replying to your questions in rotation, let me say:

1. I understand the phonograph is not now rented as it was for a number of years, but the policy of the company is to sell outright. The former rental for a phonograph with an electric battery and motor was about $7.00 per month, the company being responsible for repairs and for recharging the battery; that for a phonograph run with a treadle like a sewing machine was $3.75 per month. The motor phonograph is now sold for $180.00, including battery, and the treadle phonograph for $150.00. They are very simple in operation and easily kept in order. The one I have had in my house nearly a year has never needed any repairs except such as I could make myself in a very few

moments. My wife has learned to use it equally as well as myself. The wax cylinders or blanks upon which records are made cost $3.00 per dozen, and hold from 400 to 1,000 words each, according to the rapidity with which one dictates. After the records have been transcribed upon the typewriter, they are pared off automatically by means of a knife attached to the machine, and the blanks used as many as twenty times or more. Thus, putting the capacity at 500 words per cylinder, at a cost of $3.00 one could dictate 120,000 words. This is all the expense for operating the phonograph, except a few drops of oil each day, and the instrument ought to wear a lifetime.

Rev. Dr. Stall, associate editor of the *Lutheran Observer*, Philadelphia, chanced to read my sketch of my own work, and at once entered into correspondence with me in reference to the phonograph. He adopted it upon my recommendation, and is now using two, one at his office and one at his home, and should you write him for an expression, I am sure he would tell you he is highly delighted with its workings, and finds himself already able to do much more work than he ever dreamed of doing before. He and I occasionally exchange cylinders by mail and have the pleasure of hearing one another's voices.

At first, of course, dictating in this way is a little awkward, but as soon as one becomes used to it, it is the easiest manner of working imaginable. I find myself relieved from back-ache, strain upon the eyesight and much of the nervous tension incident to working by other methods. And as I state in my printed article, after dictating for three or four hours consecutively, I feel almost as fresh as when I sat down to the phonograph.

I believe I have answered all your inquiries, and it has given me great pleasure to do so. I shall be only too happy to render one of my favorite authors a service, which may possibly be the means of lengthening her years and enlarging her capacity for work.

A communication addressed to the North American Phonograph Company, Chicago, will bring you catalogues and all desired information as to terms of sale. If I have failed in any respect to answer your inquiries, or if any further information is desired from one who has had some practical experience with the phonograph, I am always at your service.

Again thanking you for your kindness in responding to my request, and hoping that if you test the phonograph you may find it all I have realized it to be in my experience with it, and that you will be kind enough to let me hear of it, I remain,

Very sincerely,

(Signed) J. F. COWAN.

Ties that Bind.

THE typewriter is the right hand of the stenographer, as it enables him to turn out more work in a given time, thereby increasing his earning power. Another mechanical device adds still further to his usefulness, being easier, more accurate and rapid. Need we say this device is the Edison phonograph ? The typewriter and the phonograph are therefore allied by common interests, and these excellent machines are now fast friends.

The Phonographic World says : "Notwithstanding the fact that thousands of 'shorthand writers' have been 'graduated' from hundreds of schools all over the country during the past ten years, it is as difficult in this country to secure the services of a really competent stenographer as it was ten years ago."

Poughkeepsie Enterprise.

Whenever a novelty in the field of business is placed before the public at any point, Poughkeepsie is always on the alert to secure it for the delectation of her citizens, who respond to the efforts made in their behalf by largely patronizing it.

This has been repeatedly the case in the matter of educational institutions organizing musical reunions, establishing places of amusement and entertainment, and providing remedies and medical treatment for invalids.

Recently one of Poughkeepsie's public spirited firms has gone a step further. The Smith Brothers, manufacturers of the celebrated cough drops, over a thousand tons of which are sold during the year, have erected a building containing a fine restaurant, to which is annexed a parlor for ice cream and soda water, and an elegant room with a capacity for accommodating a hundred and fifty guests, in which music is often furnished to entertain them.

The phonograph having secured a place in the esteem of the firm, this beautiful room, where costly chandeliers and paintings contribute to the enjoyment of its patrons, was obtained by Mr. George B. Lull, manager of the Automatic Exhibition Phonograph, for the New York Co., and an exhibition machine placed therein. Miss Jennie Vir Valen, of Poughkeepsie, operated this instrument, and her daily programmes were received with great delight by the audiences.

The Smith Brothers, who were at first loath to introduce the phonograph, finally agreed that it should be retained for the season, and it was not only the leading attraction, but proved to be the best paying exhibition phonograph ever displayed outside of New York City.

The popular resort of this firm is a landmark on the Hudson, and the great factory where the celebrated cough drops are manufactured is also an interesting spot to visit. It is said that the demand for these drops is so great that the factory does not begin to accommodate the hands needed to prepare them, and therefore a delivery wagon is used to distribute the drops in fifty-pound lots to the houses of

ing. These have proved efficacious. The phonograph exerted such a pleasant influence upon the guests who visited the Smith Brothers' restaurant, that it became in demand in other places in the town, and we find it in the establishment of Lucky & Platt, handled by an intelligent and swift operator, Miss Jennie Lawrence,

A Group Listening to the Phonograph at Smith Bros., Poughkeepsie.

their employees, where small pasteboard boxes are filled and labeled ready for the shipping clerk.

A ten-pound box was forwarded to Mr. Lull, to be placed in the music room of the New York Phonograph Co., where so many artists are employed to make musical records, as a remedy for the tickling in the throat produced by continued sing-

also in the hotels and in the Hudson River Railroad depot.

Mr. Eddie Gilmore made a great success of the phonograph at Highland Falls, across the river.

The enterprising firm of Smith Brothers, who first adopted the phonograph, have sent us a souvenir, in the shape of the picture herewith presented to our readers.

The Infringement of Editorial Rights.

Patience is a virtue which like its fellows must be exercised with discretion. It is not always right to "turn the other cheek" or "give the coat also "; because in the majority of questions in which we are called upon to take action, or make a decision, the rights of others besides ourselves are involved, and we are compelled to defend them at the cost of sacrificing our personal interests and desires. The ethics of any disputed matter may be changed by attending circumstances.

We are led to make these observations by reason of the gross editorial discourtesy, to call it by the mildest term, practised toward THE PHONOGRAM by the *Electrical Age*, a journal published in New York, and having its headquarters at the Pulitzer Building.

This magazine having applied to us for permission to insert on its pages the cuts published by THE PHONOGRAM and made expressly for its use, showing the offices, workshops, laboratory, etc., of Mr. Edison, at Orange, N. J., and the request being granted on *condition* that the same should be *accredited* to us, what was our surprise on beholding in the columns of *The Age*, not only the cuts, but the long article indited by the editor of THE PHONOGRAM, at a great expense of time, travel and research ; and the whole thing blazoned to the world as the handiwork of *The Electrical Age*—since it was not credited to the real author.

Now, we do not scruple to call a spade by its right name when the necessity arises for such action, and we are sustained in our course by that sterling journal *The Electrical Review*, which in a similar case, exposes (in its issue of April 1, 1893), the misdemeanor of a contemporary and metes out justice to the delinquent in terms both forcible and suitable.

In general, the editorial fraternity have exercised towards THE PHONOGRAM the respect which well-conducted sheets instinctively yield to their contemporaries, but in the few instances where a contrary course has been pursued, we have been incited to retaliate, not by a spirit of revenge, but from a sense of duty.

Directions for Adjusting "Wright" Action for Operating Phonograph in Nickel-in-the Slot Cases.

To Set Phonograph in Case.—Unscrew right-hand screw holding the plate 1 on front of top of case, swing it around and slip out the rod 2.

Take out the screws holding magnet plate at the back of the case, set in phonograph and replace above parts.

To Operate.—After making proper connections see that the brass wheel, 3, presses lightly on motor shaft wheel, and that the armature, 4, brings brass spring connections, 5, on magnet plate into electrical connection when nickel is in nickel action inside case. Also that upon release of nickel, that wheel, 3, is freed from motor shaft wheel. By adjusting at 8, screws where armature is attached to rod, pressure of brass wheel, 3, on motor shaft wheel is regulated. It is quite important this adjustment should be properly made.

When nickel is dropped into slot it makes an electrical connection which causes magnet to attract armature, 4. This brings brass plates, 5, into electrical connection, which starts phonograph. The brass wheel, 3, is brought into frictional contact with motor shaft wheel, and winds up cord attached to lever.

At bottom of lever are adjustable brass electrical contacts which release nickel, thus freeing armature and friction wheels.

To Adjust Record.—Carry the diaphragm arm over with the lever to the exact point at which it is desired needle should meet record. Adjust the connection at bottom of lever so nickel will be released at moment lever brings diaphragm over point desired on record. At the moment it is dropped out of nickel action the winding device ceases action and lever lowers diaphragm at desired point.

To adjust stopping of phonograph at proper point, place diaphragm so that needle is exactly over the end of record. Adjust the thumb screw against brass hinge, 7, behind the phonograph and current will be broken instantly when rear of

any lead slugs that are small enough to be forced through slot will drop through. This is done by the adjustment of the slot and screw at rear of iron plate fastened to block the nickel action rests on. This affects the distance between the movable brass plate and brass chute. The little piece of insulation glued to lower part of brass chute should always be in place.

The Slot.—The springs filed sharp just beneath the slot plate can be adjusted by means of the screws fastening the springs

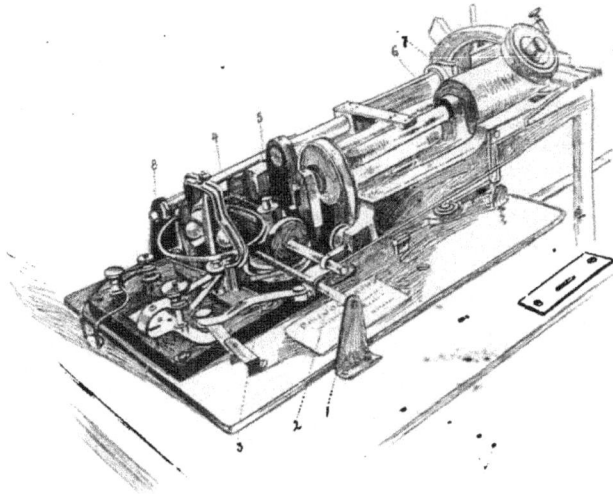

Phonograph with "Wright" Action.

diaphragm comes against this hinged connection, 1.

The above connection carries the current which runs the phonograph after it has been started by connections, 5, on magnet plate.

The device is adjusted and tested, but parts are sometimes disarranged in shipping, so that a few points regarding nickel action and slot are here given :

The Nickel Action—Admits of very fine adjustment, and can be so set that an ordinary worn nickel will operate the case, while an extremely worn nickel, and

to the fiber, and by means of filing the edge of the springs. They should be filed at such an angle as will cause the stoppage of any lead slugs the size of a nickel. Even when the springs are close together, if they are not filed at proper angles, slugs can be forced through.

Some of the contact points are brass, some silver. Clean occasionally with fine emery cloth.

Nickel lift of diaphragm arm of phonograph should be taken off.

When device is *once properly adjusted it seldom if ever needs any attention.*

Nature is God's Phonograph.

The other day I received a letter from a friend which was not at all like any other letter you ever saw. It was not written on a sheet of paper and folded in an envelope and sealed and addressed me with a stamp on one corner. It came wrapped up in soft cotton in a little wooden box, and when I opened it and saw what it was, I did not sit down and read it with my eyes as you would read a letter. But I put the brown cylinder of wax upon the spindle of a machine, which made it quickly revolve, and then inserted a couple of small tubes in my ears, and actually listened to the voice of a friend who was then over three hundred miles away in the city of Philadelphia. I heard his tones as distinctly and naturally as though he were standing by my side. It was done by the help of the wonderful Edison phonograph.

And then I thought if it is possible for a man to invent a piece of mechanism by means of which he can store up his voice in a cylinder of wax, and send it across the country hundreds of miles, or even across continents and oceans and around the world if he wished, or lay it up and have it preserved for hundreds of years so that his great, great, great, great, great-grandchildren might hear the tones of his voice, how much easier it is for God to speak to us by impressing his messages upon everything around us, so that, as David says, "Day unto day uttereth speech," and we cannot look upon a blade of grass, or the leaf of a tree, or hear the rippling brook, or the song of the bird, or the wind rustling among the leaves, without recognizing it as the voice of our heavenly Father.

All nature is God's phonograph. Ages ago He spoke into the rocks, and the diamonds and the river beds, and the coal mines, and the oil wells, and the gas wells, and some of the tones of His voice, which speaks of care and kindness for his creatures, are just being reproduced to our ears.

The wonderful Bible is another cylinder in God's phonograph. He breathed upon prophets, and kings and poets, and singers, and apostles, and the impressions made upon them were reproduced, and are still being reproduced, so that the Word of God is eternal, and nothing can destroy it, or take it away.

We shall soon begin to look for Spring. The birds will begin to fly northward, and the flowers swell and the buds upon the trees, and the sap will flow up from the roots, and the wind will blow from the south, and the snow heaps and ice melt away, the frost come out of the ground, and the earth clothe herself in beauty, but that will only be another cylinder of God's wonderful phonograph. The laws and forces which make the changes of seasons He impressed upon nature ages and ages ago, and the revelations of time bring His voice back to us. Let us try to hear God's voice all around us. Soon the earth and air will be teeming with life and beauty. He is the Author of it all.—*Our Morning Guide.*

The Columbian Exposition from a Moral, Intellectual and Political Standpoint.

The Columbian Exposition, which was intended not only to commemorate the unparalleled event from which arose the great Union of States whose prosperity is now *en evidence,* but also to afford an opportunity to the nations to judge of the progress attained by the people of this continent as compared with that of others, will serve a further purpose, possibly not designed by those originating the scheme, yet of universal importance, namely, a favorable occasion to study the effect produced upon the human race by a governmental system founded upon the principle known as a recognition of the rights of man.

Close observation of the results reached under forms of government and religion differing from those prevailing in America have led many minds to the belief that a multiplicity of laws, either constitutional or proceeding from a duly recognized source, tend to hamper and sterilize the being to whom the lordship and sovereignty of the fields and woods was given. The race in which the individual works out his own destiny untrammeled by oppression of any sort and at the same time fostered and stimulated by the genial influences and inspiring tenets of Christianity, will be the dominant one. It will do all and dare all. The land where invidious distinctions assume shape, where riches erect a barrier between man and his fellow, where the ties that should bind all humanity together as one family are ignored, will never become the leader of others.

An individual reared amid constraining influences and repressive habits of thought and action experiences upon entering the United States sensations wholly new. His ideas seem to soar, his being to be uplifted. We cannot say with Shakespeare that "he doth suffer a sea-change," yet we may borrow from a French writer the trite simile, " he has taken a new lease of life." He becomes interested in all around him : the fields, the trees, the rivers, the people are his own, and he is one of them. His eye and movements are animated, he investigates, he reasons ; someone stretches out the hand of a brother, and then he has a career before him. Soon he enters with enthusiasm into the plans and projects of friends, and, uniting with them, he exploits a mine, builds a bridge, or constructs a railway. Should his talent lie in the opposite direction he may become a votary of science, and, following the shining examples before him, invent some new system that will inure to the benefit of man,

as does the electric light, or some apparatus which, like the telegraph or phonograph, may serve as man's aid and *exponent.* His efforts to rise are not frowned upon, but encouraged. In such an atmosphere the faculties and spirit expand, and as the climatic conditions of fierce cold and fierce heat existing in America enforce activity of mind and body, he will soon perceive that the hand of nature and the hand of man conspire to stir up within him that spirit of expansion which renders the American so confident, so hopeful and so energetic.

Chicago is a noble example of American expansion ; she is the evidence of that hardihood, endurance and courage which neither conflagrations, nor tempests, nor anarchy, nor dispiriting local influences could daunt. She has pursued the work of the Columbian Exposition with a vigor and fearlessness that neither jealousy, nor apathy, nor fraud could restrain ; and verily she hath her reward.

Within her borders stands a second city, whose halls resound with the grandest music ever heard, and with the voices of saintly men and women intent upon the conquest of the human heart and the elevation of the human soul.

Here for the first time a world's congress for the advancement of "peace on earth, good will toward men " is inaugurated. Happy omen for the city of palaces, which, rising fair as a lily from the blue waves of mist-wreathed Michigan, on a plain where erstwhile only the cry of the bittern resounded along the desolate shore, now lifts her lofty domes and minarets above the aggregated wisdom, learning, riches and power of the globe, united in the single purpose of ennobling and elevating man.

--------◆◆--------

A good thing at little expense. THE PHONOGRAM for a whole year for one dollar. Now is the time to send in your subscription.

From the Crescent City.

We received from a gentleman who was visiting New Orleans during the Mardi-Gras festivities, an account of the status of the Louisiana Phonograph Co., and learn that it was never more prosperous or more buoyant than now.

The sales of machines are increasing, the people take an interest in the enterprise, and the entertainment afforded by the musical phonograph is greatly enjoyed. The musical records made by this company are of the finest. Wherever the French take up their abode one finds a grace, a perfection of detail and finish applied to the arts not met with elsewhere; and in New Orleans both the musical selections and the rendering of them is exceptionally good. Mr. Louis Vasnier's characteristic delineations of negro dialect continue very popular.

Mr. Hugh R. Conyngton is thoroughly equipped with those qualifications which make the phonograph well known in his territory.

A V(o)ice Everybody Approves Of.

"Another vice has fastened upon the American people," said a distinguished divine, who has a reputation as a humorist, in a promenade chat with The Tribune. "I refer to the phonograph habit. I confess, with more or less embarrassment, that it has taken strong hold upon me. I cannot pass one of the talking machines any more without stopping to be entertained. I fear I detect a leaning toward reproductions from the variety stage, for the temptation to let go of the nickel is strongest when the bulletin announces a bit of dialect work by the celebrated Tim Dooley, or some other star of the comedy stage. Next to that, I crave orchestral selections, though I feel that if the United States Marine and Gilmor.'s bands have filled as many phonograph cylinders as they are credited with, they must have carried phonographs on their journeys over the country, as well as sat up in the small hours at their hotels, for their alleged productions are not only numerous but full of evidences of distracting influences and fatigue upon the part of the performers. But merit aside, it is certainly agreeable to be transported in spirit from the bustle of the street to the presence of some reasonably competent caterer to the amusement of the people, and I don't much care whether I am cured of the phonograph habit or not."—*Cincinnati Tribune.*

A Soothsayer and Admonisher.

The phonograph is a dangerous thing sometimes. A girl can take it up to her room, and in her loneliness, when her sweetheart is away, she can hear all the sweet things said to her. Conversations can be handed down from generation to generation. And when the husband and wife quarrel, the wife will say, "My dear old mother warned me against you; listen to what she said," and she will pull out the family phonograph, and a wheezy noise will be heard: "You'll find him out, my dear. All men are bad. There isn't a good man living except your father —sometimes."

Prize for High School Scholars.

A prize of $5 is offered by the THE PHONOGRAM for an essay upon the phonograph written by any pupil of the high schools, within the ensuing month. It should contain not less than six hundred words nor more than one thousand, and will be subjected to the criticism of able judges.

If desired, THE PHONOGRAM will publish a short sketch of the life of the writer whose contribution is accepted, which may be sent with the article.

From the Crescent City.

We received from a gentleman who was visiting New Orleans during the Mardi-Gras festivities, an account of the status of the Louisiana Phonograph Co., and learn that it was never more prosperous or more buoyant than now.

The sales of machines are increasing, the people take an interest in the enterprise, and the entertainment afforded by the musical phonograph is greatly enjoyed.

The musical records made by this company are of the finest. Wherever the French take up their abode one finds a grace, a perfection of detail and finish applied to the arts not met with elsewhere; and in New Orleans both the musical selections and the rendering of them is exceptionally good. Mr. Louis Vasnier's characteristic delineations of negro dialect continue very popular.

Mr. Hugh R. Conyngton is thoroughly equipped with those qualifications which make the phonograph well known in his territory.

A V(o)ice Everybody Approves Of.

"Another vice has fastened upon the American people," said a distinguished divine, who has a reputation as a humorist, in a promenade chat with *The Tribune*. "I refer to the phonograph habit. I confess, with more or less embarrassment, that it has taken strong hold upon me. I cannot pass one of the talking machines any more without stopping to be entertained. I fear I detect a leaning toward reproductions from the variety stage, for the temptation to let go of the nickel is strongest when the bulletin announces a bit of dialect work by the celebrated Tim Dooley, or some other star of the comedy stage. Next to that, I crave orchestral selections, though I feel that if the United States Marine and Gilmor's bands have filled as many phonograph cylinders as they

are credited with, they must have carried phonographs on their journeys over the country, as well as sat up in the small hours at their hotels, for their alleged productions are not only numerous but full of evidences of distracting influences and fatigue upon the part of the performers. But merit aside, it is certainly agreeable to be transported in spirit from the bustle of the street to the presence of some reasonably competent caterer to the amusement of the people, and I don't much care whether I am cured of the phonograph habit or not."—*Cincinnati Tribune.*

A Soothsayer and Admonisher.

The phonograph is a dangerous thing sometimes. A girl can take it up to her room, and in her loneliness, when her sweetheart is away, she can hear all the sweet things said to her. Conversations can be handed down from generation to generation. And when the husband and wife quarrel, the wife will say, "My dear old mother warned me against you; listen to what she said," and she will pull out the family phonograph, and a wheezy noise will be heard: "You'll find him out, my dear. All men are bad. There isn't a good man living except your father —sometimes."

Prize for High School Scholars.

A prize of $5 is offered by the THE PHONOGRAM for an essay upon the phonograph written by any pupil of the high schools, within the ensuing month. It should contain not less than six hundred words nor more than one thousand, and will be subjected to the criticism of able judges.

If desired, THE PHONOGRAM will publish a short sketch of the life of the writer whose contribution is accepted, which may be sent with the article.

years. All of his dictation in stories is copied by Miss Lucille Rhodes.

* * *

George I. Miller, Superintendent of Schools, Boone, Iowa, is chairman of the executive committee for the Iowa State Teachers' Association. He has decided to have a topic on the programme at the next meeting of the association. entitled " The Phonograph and Typewriter as Educational Factors." This, certainly, will be an interesting subject and should be brought before every teachers' meeting in the country.

* * *

Mr. James L. Andem, of the Ohio Phonograph Co., has recently returned from a pleasure trip down the Mississippi as far as New Orleans. He saw many exhibitions and automatic phonographs along the larger river towns, and the owners of these machines were doing a good business and affording the residents a new and popular amusement.

Electric Devices in Berlin.

The Electrical Society of Berlin has recently experimented with a portable electric light designed to facilitate the search for the wounded on fields of battle at night. The luminous intensity is of fifty candle-power, and the battery of accumulators furnishing the electric current weighs only eight kilogrammes (sixteen pounds).

How to Succeed in this Profession.

Typewriter operators should never be satisfied with a bore acquaintance with the technique of their craft. A little knowledge is generally considered a dangerous thing, but it is extremely useful in conjunction with typewriting. At all events, it is better than none at all. Some knowledge of German and French is especially useful.

A Leading New York Merchant.

To found an extensive commercial house is to render a service to one's country. It is a part of our nation's progress. To this end many requisites are necessary. Industry and perseverance are the first principles. Next, an attractive personality; again, integrity of character, and, finally, that mental grasp which enables a man to carry out in detail the large generalities that constitute the soul of his trade.

The history of the establishment of A. Raymond & Co., of New York. is a history of extensive intercourse with the world of commerce and of high achievement. Its supreme success constitutes one of the reasons why this illustrated article is presented to the public in this centennial year.

Mr. Aaron Raymond, the head of the firm, was born in 1834, in Bedford, Westchester County, New York. Educated in the academy there, he came to the metropolis, and engaged with a firm on Cortlandt street, with which he remained for six years. The times were propitious, and on May 1, 1857, he became a partner of the firm known as Rogers & Raymond. It occupied a building at the corner of Nassau and Fulton street. Since then it has become a magnificent edifice, that faces both Nassau and Fulton and extends from Fulton to Ann street. It is an historical locality. Before the war the *New York Herald* was printed immediately opposite, and the presence of the elder James Gordon Bennett and the hundreds of public men who formed the circle of his acquaintance, was a familiar spectacle. Opposite, on Fulton street, was the *New York Daily Sun*, then edited by Moses Y. Beach. Afterwards the *Commercial Advertiser*, one of the oldest papers in New York, made this site its home until a conflagration destroyed the time-honored property, and a modern commercial building occupies the spot. The establishment of A. Raymond & Co. is probably better known to the citizens of New York than any other of its kind in the metropolis. Situated directly on the line of travel from Broadway to the Brooklyn Ferry, millions of people have passed the locality, and it goes without saying that the handsome and varying display of novelties in the great show windows on Nassau and Fulton streets constituted a landmark for the older residents and are familiar and popular with the new generation. Many changes have been made obedient to the growth of trade and the demand of progression in the business world. Their inviting entrances proclaim a welcome to the public. Entering the men's furnishing department from Nassau street the visitor will be struck by the magnificent taste exhibited in the arrangement for the display of goods. The room is like a great hall. The show cases and fixtures are of solid ash, the former being fitted with plates of beveled glass. Incandescent lamps shed a brilliant radiance, and the rainbow-like hues of silken stuffs, reflected from shining folds on every hand, added to the infinite variety of color, form, and shape of fabrics included in the term "furnishings," are well calculated to bewilder even a connoisseur. No less than fifty electric lights in this immense room, each of sixteen-candle power, furnish a brilliancy that is at all times attractive to the eye. It is not without purpose that these lavish decorations have been provided at so much expense. They constitute a fitting framework to the costly material exhibited. The main floor is arranged for the display of an immense

Aaron Raymond.

stock of tailor-made clothing, comprising all grades and styles, and readily fitted to every patron, no matter what may be his size. These goods are all made under the inspection of experts who give no less attention to the lowest priced garments than they do to the most expensive. The hat department is also located on this floor, where the latest ideas in men's headware are displayed in attractive and liberal profusion.

A commodious stairway leads to the basement, which is neatly furnished and fitted for the display of a portion of their offerings. Incandescent lamps adorn the ceiling, and shed a counterfeit of daylight which is equal to Nature's best. An exhaustive shoe department occupies one portion, trunks and bags another, the large dimensions remaining being devoted to athletic, gymnasium and bicycle suits and accessories, which are shown in great variety. Passing to the second floor you are in the custom department, which occupies the entire space excepting the portion devoted to the private offices. This room is fitted with windows upon three sides, and "as light as day" would be

vise and cut the great number of garments that are subsequently manufactured into stylish clothing for a generous patronage. The fifth and sixth floors are devoted to the storing of reserve stock, both in piece goods and ready-made garments.

R.ymond's Building. Corner Fulton and Nassau Streets.

correct in describing it. Incandescent lamps prevail here also, but are seldom brought into requisition. The third floor is used for active stock in passing from the receiving room to the retail departments. The fourth floor is where the designers and artists are located, who de-

It is one of the rules of Mr. Raymond that no patron ever shall leave his establishment dissatisfied. If after purchase he does not like an article, he may change or return it at will and get his money back. The salesmen are genteel and courteous, and even though the visitor may not be a purchaser, he will receive the same affable treatment as if he had been among the most liberal patrons. A special feature of the establishment may be designated as the special order department, from which is systematically sent out to the neighboring cities and towns a complete set of samples of goods mounted on cardboard and consisting of the rarest textures for overcoats, suits and trousers of both foreign and domestic manufacture. In this way the customer is enabled to order from his own home, from Raymond & Co., whatever he may desire in their line, and be assured that his requirements will be fulfilled to the smallest detail. In fact, it is the business of the firm to please and supply its patrons without the incidental expenses involved in a visit to New York. Among the features of the establishment is the publication of *Raymond's Monthly*, a lively magazine that keeps pace with the changes of style and pattern and leaves nothing to be desired on the part of any citizen, young or old, whose aim it is, so far as his clothes are concerned, to be like " one to the manor born."

The phonograph also plays no inconspicuous part. The large correspondence that forms a part of a counting-room business of many of our New York firms has made this grand device of our great chief Edison a necessity. The more a merchant uses it, the more he is disinclined to part with it. It dispenses with the employment of two or three clerks in writing his letters, and, in brief, it becomes his confidential friend, with whom the children of his brain linger forever.

The African and the Phonograph.

As a promoter of merriment the talking machine is a success. Wags of all nationalities avail themselves of its apparently occult powers to puzzle or baffle the unsuspecting and the simple, while the volatile son of Erin, the breezy Westerner, the shrewd Down-Easter and the oracular Ethiopian are in turn its victims or its exploiters.

Mr. Joel Chandler Harris relates in his inimitable style a series of practical jokes perpetrated by means of a phonograph on the colored citizen who figures extensively in many of his humorous narratives under the pseudonym of " Uncle Remus," and as they are of recent occurrence, and therefore have not yet had time to " swing around the circle " of all the great dailies in the country, we introduce them here.

One of the ladies of a certain household where the old African had held the post of retainer for many years, having obtained a phonograph and familiarized herself with the mode of operating it, conceived the idea of exhibiting it to the ancient servitor. Calling him up, she instructed him to apply the tube to his ears and listen to the sounds from the instrument. The announcement of a piece in a hard, metallic voice gave Uncle Remus a nervous shock which was expressed by a look at the lady and quick rolling of the eyes.

After that, a musical arrangement played by a band proceeded from the instrument, and he seemed to enjoy it immensely. When the music terminated with the usual crash, he took the tubes from his ears and examined them attentively ; finding nothing inside, he inserted them in his ears again, but, of course, heard nothing. Then he interrogated the lady, whom he calls " Miss Sally," desiring to " learn whar'bouts does dese pipes lead to."

" Right here to the phonograph."

" De which 'em ? "

" This little machine here."

" Uh ! Miss Sally. Dey may fool you, but dey can't fool me. De t'er een 'er dese here pipes ain't so might' fer from de circus. I dunner whar'bouts de circus is, but wharsomever de show's gwine on, right dar is de t'ereen er dem are pipes. You ax Marse John dar, en ef he aint playin' no prank on yer, 'long er dish yer contraption, he'll tell yer de same. When I go home ta-night I gwine ter to holler at my ole woman : 'You, Katherin, wake up fum dar, where you settin' noddin' by de chimbly jam. You say yo' Miss Sally de smartest white woman in de Nunited States er Georgay, and yit she is done been fooled by dem town folks.' Dat des zackly what I'm gwine to tell er, and I boun' you Marse John'll b'ar me out in it ; won't you ?''

Uncle Remus rattled this off so fast that the lady had no opportunity to explain, but at last she showed him the cylinder, telling him that it was covered with wax and the music was written on the wax.

He scrutinized the cylinder after putting on his spectacles, then looked closely at Miss Sally and remarked :

" Miss Sally, I bin knowin' you sence you waz a little bit er baby, en hain't never hear you gwine on dis a way befo'. I wish you'd please'm tell me how dat ar brass ban' gwine git in dar? De ban' what I hear in dese here pipes had de big horn en de base drum in it yit, let lone all de yuther horns, en my min' pintedly tells me dat ef day wuz all to git in dat ar shebang dar, dey'd bust it wide open. Now you know dat yo'self, Miss Sally."

The lady wished to laugh, but controlled herself, and adjusted another cylinder, telling the old man to place the tubes in his ears. It was the banjo solo, and when it was concluded Uncle Remus exclaimed : " What I tell you, Miss Sally ? I knowed dar was a show goin' on roun' yer. Dar was de man pickin' de banjo, and' doin' like he hear folks say de niggers does. I ken shet my eyes en' see 'im right now. He got blackin' on his face, en' his

eyes is mo' blood shotten den what nigger's eyes is. He got on high stovepipe hat, en' he show de bottom of his shoe wid chalk marks on it. He ain't no mo' like a nigger den a bumble bee is like a roan mule. Yit dar he sets and plunks on de banjer. Marse John," the old man went on, "you reckon Miss Sally gwine ter up'n low dat dat ar man wid de banjer is in de beeswax ? "

For answer, " Marse John " winked his eye, and shook his head with an air of mystery. Meanwhile, " Miss Sally" was adjusting the chimes of Trinity. Uncle Remus, listening, winked his eyes at every stroke of the bells, and remarked, when the ringing ceased :

" Is anybody ever hear de beat o' dat? Ef dey aint a big fire broke out som'rs, de meetin'-houses is all got in a bunch. Dat ar beesewax got a mighty tough job of it, to hol' all dem bells." .

Then came a conversation between Uncle Remus and the cook, which had been spoken into the phonograph by Miss Sally. The old man's placid countenance gathered severity as the dialogue was poured into his ears. The lady's imitation of the cook was cleverer than she intended, and when Uncle Remus hung the tubes across the machine there was an ominous frown on his brow. " Where are you going ? " asked Miss Sally, as the old man started out.

" I'm gwine out dar an' see dat nigger 'ooman. Dat ar contraption is wuss den runnin' de kyards. Hit beats eaves-drappin'. Hit tell you what folks been sayin', arter dey done said it an' gone. Dat nigger 'ooman dar in de kitchen been talkin' 'bout me scan'lous."

With that Uncle Remus went out in the back yard, and those in the house heard a conversation something like this :

" I ain't been talkin' 'bout you needer. She tell you dat? She 'uz just prankin' wid you."

"Miss Sally ain't tell me nothin' 'tall.
I hear de ve'y words wid my own years."

"Looker here, nigger man ; is yer
gwine crazy ? Ef yer is, I want yer ter
g'way f'm here."

"You up'n tell Miss Sally dat I been
stealin' tater pie en fried sassidge en light
bread."

"Is she tell you dat ?"

— "Miss Sally ain't tell me nuthin. I
tuck'n hear de ve'y words. What you
done wid dat apern full er biscuits you
tuck'n slipped off wid las night? An
whar dat can er develish ham, en dat ar
bag er prunes, en dem ar sparribs what
you kyard off day fo yistiddy?"

"I ain't deff. What you wanter be
hollerin so loud fer ? She don't want
to hear you gwine on dat ar way. All de
white folks wants is to git de niggers to
quoilin' en fightin' en see em go to de
chain-gang. You hush up and go on
'bout yo' business."

A little later when Miss Sally was attending to affairs in the dining-room, the
cook took occasion to remark :

"Miss Sally, you better make dat ole
nigger man keep his mouf offen me. I'm
gwine cripple him, mon, if he don't
lemme 'lone. Is you hear what he tell
me dis evenin' ?"

"What was it?" asked the lady,
feigning ignorance.

"He come out here, he did," said the
cook, scornfully, "and say dat I wuz settin'
my cap fer him, case you all had 'im in
de settin'-room dar, showin im de picters.
He de sassiest ole nigger I ever is see."

Exhibition of the Phonograph in the Auditorium of the Drexel Institute, Philadelphia, Pa., March 9, 1893.

A notice of this interesting event was
published in our last issue, but we had
not then received a full account of what
took place on the occasion, and therefore
lay before our readers to-day the excellent
description just furnished us by Mr. Mil-
ton F. Adams, who, in connection with
Mr. E. P. Wallace, local manager of the
North. American Phonograph Co., of
Philadelphia, had charge of the exhibition.

Despite inclement weather, there were
present at least one thousand persons, in-
cluding some of the most prominent people in Philadelphia. It was a complete
success in every way. Its principal object
was to demonstrate the commercial value
of the phonograph, but it included musical numbers and recitations.

Cornetist Wm. H. Distin played into the
phonograph numerous airs, among which,
by request, were the "Sewanee River,"
"Non e Ver," "The Palms." These airs
were then reproduced on another instrument, to the immense delight of the audience. The orchestral records included
the "Miserere," "Il Trovatore," and the
"Toreador Song," from the opera of Car-
men.

Several young ladies sang into the
phonograph ; their songs were reproduced
on another machine with very great success. Seven phonographs and five typewriters were used at this exhibition.

Messrs. Adams and Wallace practically
demonstrated from the platform the commercial advantages and uses of the phonograph, dictated several business letters to
it, which were transcribed by expert
operators and distributed throughout the
hall.

Mr. Du Bois, of the Philadelphia Trust
and Safe Deposit Co., spoke for the audience and stated that the commercial advantages of the phonograph could not be
too highly extolled ; that from practical
experience in his office he had found that
typewriters had no trouble in understand-
ing (or hearing) all that was dictated to
the phonograph.

Mr. Joshua L. Bailey, the well-known
dry-goods merchant, recited a humorous

tale into the phonograph, on the subject of the age of the public buildings in Philadelphia, which was then reproduced on another machine to the very great gratification of the audience. Mr. Bailey was evidently very popular as an exhibitor.

A three-foot paper horn was experimented upon for recording, and with very good success, particularly in the matter of cornet solos.

The exhibition was so successful that Professor James McAllister, superintendent of Drexel Institute, has decided that a phonograph shall be an important adjunct to the Department of Physics of the Institute.

Extraction of Caoutchouc (Indian Rubber) from Turpentine.

Mr. Tilden demonstrated some years ago that the oil of turpentine contains isoprene, one of the products obtained from the distillation of caoutchouc, and which, treated with powerful acids, is converted into a solid elastic mass showing all the properties of india-rubber.

Bourhardet had already observed the fact that heat would produce the same transformation on isoprene, which would seem to indicate that this substance is the caoutchouc pure.

Natural caoutchouc, the same as artificial caoutchorc, appears to be formed of two elements, one of which is more soluble than the other. The dissolution of artificial caoutchouc leaves, by evaporation, a residue which presents the same characteristics as the residue left by a dissolution of natural caoutchouc. Further, this artificial caoutchouc combines with sulphur under the same conditions as the natural caoutchouc.

The *Electrician* remarks that this discovery will give occasion for important industrial applications.—*Revue Scientifique.*

Rare Pictures for Sale.

The inventions of Mr. Thomas A. Edison have contributed so largely to human comfort and happiness that it would be safe to say that one-half of the population of the world has partial knowledge of him through his works ; and a considerable portion of the visitors to the World's Fair who witness daily the usefulness of these will be desirous of acquiring an accurate presentment of the form and features of the great inventor.

They can accomplish this object by applying at the office of THE PHONOGRAM, Room 87, Pulitzer Building, New York City, where photographs of Mr. Edison. taken at various periods of his life, and of his home, library and laboratory, etc., are to be found. Both those who come to America and those who do not may be furnished with these likenesses by sending an order through the advertisement in THE PHONOGRAM. These photographs are copyrighted, and have been obtained from a source not open to the general public. They are the best ever taken.

A New Field for Bread Winners.

One of our exchanges, *The Counting House,* Leiscester, England, has given some very pertinent ideas in regard to the typewriter which are equally applicable and valuable to users of the phonograph :

" New inventions of a practical kind always create a new demand for labor. New tools have to be made before the new machine can be efficiently manufactured. New powers are called forth for their construction, as for that of the machine itself. The invention, when placed on the market and brought into common use, opens a new field of employment to those who can manipulate it." This is especially so of the phonograph.

AUTHORS AND PUBLISHERS.

The Life of Thomas A. Edison.

BY A. AND W. K. L. DICKSON.

Every intelligent person who is able to command the time necessary to follow the general current of thought as expressed in the literature of the present age, must be struck by the manifest tendency of that current to flow through the domain of science, seeking to penetrate its mysteries and grasp its laws.

This inclination is so marked, that books of fiction and even "belles lettres" are for the most part, relegated to younger minds, and publications dispensing information relating to the vast circle of sciences alone find favor with the majority of readers.

We view this phase of civilization as far as it concerns our national existence, with profound satisfaction. According to our belief it is the precursor of a higher ascent in the scale of progress and sentiment. The test of the world's advancement is the measure of learning attained by the great family of man.

Real knowledge, that is, an insight into the structure and component parts of the planet on which we dwell, the forces of nature, an approximate comprehension of the complex machinery of the firmament above us, leads to the perception of spiritual truth. If the Jews had not been too much immersed in the contemplation of things temporal, the discussion of doctrinal subtleties, the adherence to ceremonial law, the vagaries of the sophist, no occasion would have arisen for Pilate's inquiry, "What is truth?" When a nation engages in the quest for truth, it is sure to find it; the looking for it is evidence that man possesses faculties enabling him to recognize it when found.

America, even in her youth, has manifested a proclivity to grapple with knotty problems; and now in her prime she presses onward to the race toward learning with Quixotic enthusiasm. She has produced many ripe scholars and statesmen, and astronomy, physics, electrical, nautical and kindred sciences have been materially enriched by her sons.

In these latter days, the prolific brain and executive ability of our famed inventor Thomas A. Edison, have combined to erect a standard of scholarship in electrical science which few men with the exception of Lord Kelvin, have reached. We opine that the universal interest in learning, entertained by Americans, has been an important factor in impelling this eminent person towards the goal he has attained.

We have been led to expatiate on this theme by reason of a recent perusal of the biographical sketch of Mr. Edison contained in *Cassier's Magazine*, emanating from the pen of writers who are able to do justice to the subject.

With the skill of a Vernet, they have worked in on the canvas the events of his life with such inimitable art, that the effect upon the soul is indelible. One is puzzled to decide which has produced the greater impression, the story or its hero. Logic, rhetorical skill, artistic training, and intuitive knowledge of the laws of taste have all combined to stamp this as a model of excellent biography.

* * *

The Review of Reviews for April, 1893, is rich in original matter and contains highly interesting resumés of themes treated in contemporary magazines. Among others furnished from the pen of one of its own corps of writers is the article on the President of the United States and the members of his cabinet, a timely subject and affording abundance of fact which will be new to most of the readers of this magazine.

The likeness of Vice-President Stevenson is a gem in the way of photographic art, and the artist who reproduced it in *The Review* shows his appreciation of excellence by presenting it with the minutest muscular tracery of the face apparent, which in portraits should always accompany accurate drawing of the outlines.

* * *

The History of Art in Antiquity is the title of a work that cannot fail to be of value to all scientists and lovers of learning, since the means employed to obtain an exhaustive disquisition on this alluring theme have been largely adequate to the end. A notice of the publication appears in the Supplement to the *Revue Scientifique* (March 11, 1893), and it is issued from the Librarie Hachette et Cie., Boulevard 79, Paris.

Adverting to the grounds upon which this scholarly and extensive history was undertaken, we learn from the writer, who expatiates on its claims to public attention and admiration, that it has been conjointly produced by men occupying high positions under the government of France and Members of the French Institute. Two of these, Messrs. Perrot and Chipiez, have received government prizes in connection with the task they have completed by producing these volumes, and the former returned to Greece two years ago for the purpose of visiting, with Messrs. Schliemann and Doerpfold, the sites of Troy, of Tyrinthe and Mycènes, where the surprising discoveries were made, the results of which are made known in the volume just about to be published, which is designated *Primitive Greece—Mycènian Art.*

The entire work will comprise eight volumes.

Plan to Forward the Interests of the People in the Matter of Common Roads.

We approach this subject with enthusiasm ; it has weighed upon our minds for a long time, and we shall be happy to lend whatever influence we possess towards promoting all legal measures necessary to accomplish the good work.

Those who need good roads are the people residing in the country or in small towns, and they constitute the majority of the inhabitants of the United States. Most of them produce directly or indirectly all they eat and wear. If their labor is given to the actual conducting of farms, the losses to them occasioned by bad roads are extremely heavy, for small proprietors and tenants cannot afford to send produce by rail to market, and even wealthy farmers are frequently overwhelmed by the burdens of railroad transportation of crops or manufactured products.

This is an axiom. Therefore let us bring the wisdom of the past to our aid in considering this question, and it may help us to find a remedy for the evil.

Years ago, that able and astute statesman, the Hon. John Bright, presented his views on the transportation of farm products and the home-made productions of skilled laborers, to a convenient market, before the British Parliament, in connection with the condition of Her Majesty the Queen of England's subjects in India. Numbers of the Hindoo race convey the fruits of their toil to a market by means of waterways, and at that time these required attention and repairs from the Government. Mr. Bright discussed the matter at great length in all its aspects, and the force of his arguments and the confidence he inspired by his character and knowledge of political economy was sufficient to enable him to gain his point and bring redress to the suffering natives of Hindostan. Thenceforth their merchandise or crops were boated safely and easily to the commercial havens they sought.

This desideratum should be provided in our own country by constructing good highways for the use of the people. It should be remembered that in the United States there is very little sterile soil. The proportion of rocky, sandy and boggy land as compared to the fertile and arable area is small. And the very richness and fertility is the source of difficulties ; since it is easy to hew out a rough, yet firm roadway in the forest, where the earth is tenacious or gravelly under the feet ; but when one encounters the mud and ooze of Louisiana, Mississippi, Arkansas and Alabama, or the black, waxy soil of Texas, or the red clay of North Carolina and Virginia, where the wheels sink to the hub and have to be pried out with levers, the question of making or keeping roads in repair assumes another hue. Statesmen, and voters likewise, should remember that good roads are not a luxury, but a necessity, and that *railways* can *never fill their place.* And they should furthermore recollect that the agricultural contributions of those great States have been the direct cause of growth and fruitful source of wealth to all the large cities in the Atlantic seaboard ; which, without such sustenance, would now only count their population by thousands instead of millions.

Mr. Albert A. Pope, of Boston, has published in pamphlet form a copy of a petition which he has been mainly instrumental in framing, and which is signed by many distinguished men of the Republic, memorializing Congress to move in the matter of establishing a special department for preparing students to fit themselves correctly to construct roads, and also to exhibit models of road building for the use of the States.

We wish his undertaking all the success it deserves, and believe that proper movement in this direction will insure blessings to the people, at present undreamed of, just as this influx of money through trade has rendered possible so many inventions, among others, that of the Phonograph.

TRADE NOTES.

The Columbia Typewriter Manufacturing Co. are preparing a fine exhibition at the World's Fair. One machine will be finished in gold and one in silver. This company is building a large factory on 116th street, to meet the increasing demands of their business.

* * *

The New England Phonograph Co. have always something new and interesting. Write for their catalogue.

* * *

The ordinary prices of typewriters are cut in two at the Typewriters' Exchange, 10 Barclay street. You can also exchange your old machine for a new one—any make.

* * *

"A word to the wise is sufficient." Successful dealers use Underwood's typewriter ribbons.

* * *

Every phonograph agent should order songs from H. J. Wehman, 130 Park Row. They will bring you dollars where you invest cents. See advertisement.

* * *

Everybody interested in the phonograph and musical records should read the advertisement of the New Jersey Phonograph Co., Newark, in this issue.

World's Fair Hotel Accommodations,

And Headquarters for Shorthand Writers, Typewriter Operators,
Phonograph Operators and Wheelmen.

Are you Coming?   Where will you Stay?   What will you Pay?

The hotel is entirely new ; is provided with every modern convenience, and will accommodate fully two thousand guests. It is within fifteen minutes ride of the grounds, via the Illinois Central R. R., and within two blocks of the depot. Special attention will be given, and provision made for ladies, both old and young, who may visit the exposition without escorts. Rooms, when secured in advance, may be obtained at rates varying from 50 cents each a day for four persons to $1.50 a day for one person. The Company has made arrangements for a large hotel at the Fair grounds, where lunch may be taken, and Wheelmen store their wheels.

Persons wishing to obtain full information how to secure rooms and board in advance, should address the WORLD'S FAIR ACCOMMODATION CO., 56 Fifth Avenue, Chicago, Ill., enclosing stamp for pamphlet.

Prof. F. S. Humphrey, the well-known stenographer and author, will look after the interests of the shorthanders, typewritists, and wheelmen.

TEN REASONS WHY

EDISON'S PHONOGRAPH

IS SUPERIOR TO ANY STENOGRAPHER.

1. SPEED.

You can dictate as rapidly as you please, and are never asked to repeat.

2. CONVENIENCE.

You dictate alone, at any hour of day or night that suits your convenience.

3. SAVING OF OPERATOR'S TIME.

During dictation operator can be employed with other work. Operators make twice the speed in writing out that is possible from shorthand notes.

4. ACCURACY.

The phonograph can only repeat what has been said to it.

5. INDEPENDENCE.

You are independent of your operator. It is easy to replace a typewriter operator, but a competent stenographer is hard to find.

6. ECONOMY.

The cost of an outfit added to salary of operator is less than that of a stenographer, and results obtained far superior.

7. SIMPLICITY.

The method is so simple that no time need be lost in learning it. You can commence work AT ONCE.

8. TIRELESSNESS.

The phonograph needs no vacation. Does not grumble at any amount of over-work.

9. PROGRESSIVENESS.

The most progressive business houses are now using phonographs, and indorse them enthusiastically.

10. SUB-DIVISION OF LABOR.

In cases where you have a number of letters or a long document, necessitating several cylinders, same can be equally distributed among your typewriters, a saving of both time and labor.

PRICE LIST AND SIZES

—OF—

PHOTOGRAPHS

—OF—

Mr. Thomas A. Edison,

LABORATORY, ETC., ETC.

Pictures, 11x14 on 14x17 cards, price $2.00 each, or $22.00 per dozen.

No. 1. Laboratory exterior—winter scene.
" 2.   "   Galvanometer or Electrical Dept.
" 3.   "   Phonograph, Experimental "
" 4.   "   Chemical Dept.
" 5. Mr. Edison at work in Chemical Dept.
" 6. Laboratory main machine shop.
" 7.   "   exter. (summer) corner rear view.
" 8.   "   Library, with statue " Genius of Light."
" 9. " Glenmont," exter., showing Conservatory and " Den."
" 10. " Glenmont," Parlor.
" 11.   "   " Den," showing ceiling painting, upright view.
" 12. " Glenmont," " Den," horizontal view.
" 13.   "   exter., showing Conservatory and porch.
" 14. Edison sitting at Laboratory table, taken 1892.
" 15. Edison portrait, oval, with signature, 1889.
" 16. Edison Listening to Phonograph, 11 x 14.
" 17. Statue in Library, "Genius of Light."
" 18. Laboratory Dynamo Dept.
" 19.   "   exter., main building.
" 20. The Edison Phonograph, latest type.
" 21. Laboratory, Precision Dept., upper shop.
" 22.   "   exter., summer, same view as No. 1.
" 23. Edison's portrait at 14.
" 24.   "   mother.
" 25.   "   portrait at 4.
" 26. Allegorical painting—Birth of the Edison Incandescent Lamp, Menlo Park, 1875.
" 27. Edison's Birthplace.
" 28. Group of Night Workers, with Edison at Phonograph.
" 29. Laboratory's renowned Stock Room.
" 30. Pattern and Carpenter Shop.
" Edison talking to phono. (profile.)

Pictures, 8x10 on 10x12 cards, price $1.25, and $14.00 per dozen.

No. 40. " Grand Trunk Herald," printed and published by T. A. Edison on board train Chicago & Grand Trunk R.R., at 14, front view.
" 41. " Grand Trunk Herald," printed and published by T. A. Edison on board train Chicago & Grand Trunk R.R., at 14, back view.

No. 42. Edison's Birthplace.
" 43.   "   Profile, ½ figure.
" 44. Edison's bust, oval, with autograph, 1889.
" 46. Edison, ⅓ length, 1889.
" 47. Llewellyn Park Entrance.
" 48. Edison at 14.
" 49.   "   listening to Phonograph.
" 50. Edison's Mother.
" 51.   "   First Patent, Vote Recorder, Patent sheet.
" 52. Edison's Newark Ward St. Factory, Edison in group, 1876.
" 53. Edison at 4.
" 54. Allegorical Painting.—Birth of the Edison Incandescent Lamp—Menlo Park, 1878.
" 55. Edison driving his first Electric Locomotive, 1879.

Pictures, 5 x 8 on 8 x 10 cards, price $1.00, or $11.00 per dozen.

No. 60. Edison's Birthplace.
" 61. Edison, ¼ size, 1889.
" 62.   "   bust, oval, autograph attached, 1892.
" 63. Edison's bust, oval, autograph attached, 1889.
" 64. Laboratory, a corner of Library.
" 65. " Glenmont," exter. view, from road fence.
" 66. The Edison Phonograph—latest type.
" 67. Precision Dept., upper shop, (laboratory.)
" 68. Laboratory Library, with Ferns.
" 69. Edison Phonograph Works.
" 70. Edison's Mother.
" 71.   "   "   reduced size.
" 72. Edison at 14.
" 73.   "   " 4.

MISCELLANEOUS.

No. 100. Micro-photo., Fly's head, 6¼x8¼, $1.35.
" 101.   "   Bamboo Filaments, showing Fibro-Vascular bundles, used in Edison Lamps, 6¼x8¼, $1.35.
" 102. Micro-photo., Bamboo Filaments, showing Fibro-Vascular bundles, used in Edison Lamps, greater magnification, 6¼x8¼, $1.35.
" 150. Llewellyn Park Entrance, 10x12, $1.50.
Many other Photo-Micrographs.

Please order by number, giving size.

Address. **V. H. McRAE,** "Phonogram," World **Building, N. Y.**